POCKET GARDENING GUIDES

SHRUBS AND SMALL TREES

DAVID SQUIRE

POCKET GARDENING GUIDES

SHRUBS AND SMALL TREES

DAVID SQUIRE

Illustrated by Vana Haggerty

TIGER BOOKS INTERNATIONAL
LONDON

Designed and conceived by

THE BRIDGEWATER BOOK COMPANY LTD

Art Directed by PETER BRIDGEWATER

Designed by TERRY JEAVONS

Illustrated by VANA HAGGERTY FLS

Edited by MARGOT RICHARDSON

CLB 3370

This edition published in 1994 by

TIGER BOOKS INTERNATIONAL PLC, London

Printed and bound in Singapore

ISBN 1-85501-385-1

CONTENTS

In search of plants	6–7
Commercial values	8–9
International survey	10–11
Buying shrubs and trees	12–13
Preparing and planning a shrub border	14–15
Planting a container-grown shrub	16–17
Planting a bare-rooted shrub or tree	18–19
Planting a hedge	20–21
Looking after trees and shrubs	22–23
Pruning deciduous shrubs	24–25
Pruning evergreen shrubs	26–27
Winter-flowering shrubs and trees	28–29
Spring-flowering shrubs and trees	30–31
Early summer-flowering shrubs and trees	32–33
Late summer-flowering shrubs and trees	34–35
Coloured leaves	36–37
Coloured barks and shoots	38–39
Autumn-coloured leaves	40–41
Berries and fruits	42–43
Scented shrubs and trees	44–45
Foliage hedges	46–47
Flowering hedges	48–49
Small conifers	50–51
Large conifers	52–53
Shrubs and trees for coastal areas	54–55
Shrubs and trees for acid soils	56–57
Chalky soils	58–59
Tree and shrub calendar	60–61
Useful shrub and tree terms	62–63
Index	64

IN SEARCH OF PLANTS

THE *English naturalist Sir Joseph Banks (1743–1820) was instrumental in sending out plant hunters from the Royal Botanic Gardens, Kew.*

PERHAPS the earliest known account of plant-collecting expeditions dates from when Queen Hatshepsut of Egypt, in 1495 BC, sent out a group to Somalia (then known as the Land of the Punt) to bring back living specimens of trees whose resin yielded frankincense. There are records that thirty-one young trees were collected, and brought back in baskets slung on poles and carried by slaves.

Although Africa may have been the first foreign area visited by European plant hunters, equatorial Africa was the last sight for many nineteenth-century botanists: few Europeans survived the malaria-carrying mosquitoes.

ON THE SHRUB TRAIL

As more territories were opened up, botanists and nurserymen explored them in search of new plants. But of all areas, North America, Japan and China must be the richest in shrubs and trees.

North America was opened up first, with discoverers travelling freely: William Clark and Merriwether Lewis first crossed the country, but plant hunting in the western states began much later.

However, some areas of Alaska had earlier been botanized by the Russians, and plants taken to the Botanic Garden at St. Petersburg (later Leningrad).

During the sixteenth century, the 'intolerance and cruelty' of Spanish and Portuguese missionaries had caused Japan to close its borders

CAPTAIN *William Bligh (1754–1817) is chiefly known for the mutiny on his ship the* Bounty *in 1789 when endeavouring to take Breadfruit from Tahiti to the West Indies.*

Artocarpus communis

DURING *their journey across North America in the early 1800s, the Captains William Clark and Merriwether Lewis found many plants, including the Oregon Grape* (Mahonia aquifolium), *an evergreen shrub now widely grown in temperate climates. The thicket-forming Snowberry* (Symphoricarpos albus) *is another popular shrub they discovered.*

MANY *trees, shrubs and climbers now widely grown in our gardens originated in the East. The bushy climber* Clematis macropetala *comes from Siberia and Northern China, while the early-summer flowering* Viburnum plicatum *is from Japan and China. The Rose of China (*Hibiscus rosa-sinensis*) originated in China.*

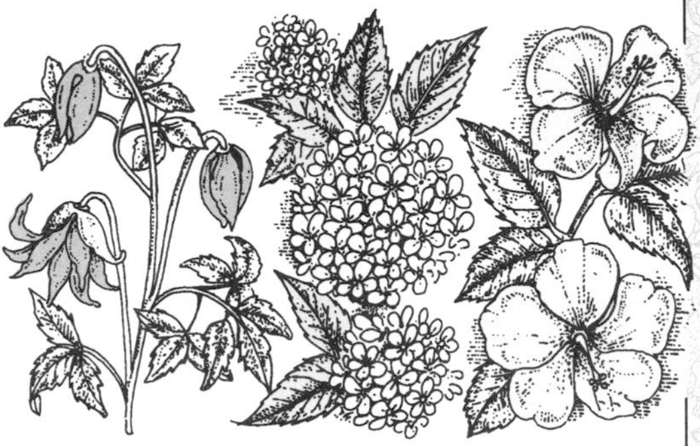

ACROSS NORTH AMERICA

Between 1804 and 1806, the Captains William Clark and Merriwether Lewis made their celebrated transcontinental crossing of North America. It had been planned a year earlier, but had to be delayed until the conclusion of the Louisiana Purchase, when Thomas Jefferson bought a major part of North America from Napoleon for $15 million.

The world-famous Veitch nursery then sent out plant hunters who returned with treasures such as the Star Magnolia (*Magnolia stellata*). Other shrubs to come from Japan include *Hydrangea paniculata grandiflora* and *Elaeagnus pungens*.

Chinese plants began to filter through, overland to Europe, at an early date. Europeans, however, were never welcome in China, although borders were not actually closed until 1755. It was not until the end of the Opium Wars of 1840–42 that entry ports were opened up.

to visitors, and the only people with whom they would trade were the Chinese and Dutch, who sent no missionaries and traded only from Deshima, an artificial island in the port of Nagasaki. It was not until 1854 that Japan began to open up its borders again. This was partly as a result of Philipp Franz von Siebold's involvement with the Dutch East India Company and later when he acted as a consultant to the Japanese Privy Council, in part to advise on the introduction of European sciences. He introduced many plants to Europe through the Dutch nursery Siebold and Co. From there they were taken to many other countries.

BRING THEM BACK ALIVE!

Travelling through foreign countries could be rewarded with the discovery of new plants. Many were transported back as seeds and a barrel-like cask (above) was used to help germinate them on long voyages. But most discoveries were of growing plants. Wardian Cases, developed by Dr. Nathaniel Ward during the 1820s, helped to 'get them back alive'.

COMMERCIAL VALUES

GARDENERS usually view trees and shrubs as attractive features, brightening borders throughout the year or creating focal points. Many, however, are better known for their commercial value, especially when providing a country's main source of income, such as coffee.

The commercial values of trees and shrubs are impressively wide. Several of their products are now created artificially, but during the nineteenth century they had many values and much research was carried out by botanical gardens to consider further uses, none more so than at the Royal Botanic Gardens, Kew, London.

MANY AND VARIED USES

The range of shrubs and trees that have been used commercially is impressively wide – including many differing purposes:

- Rubber: Many trees yield rubber, including the Rubber Tree (*Ficus elastica*), so often grown as a houseplant in temperate regions. Indeed, it was one of the earliest sources of rubber and originally used for erasers. But it was *Hevea brasiliensis*, native to Brazil, that eventually proved to be the best commercial source.
- Gutta-percha: Similar to rubber and produced by several tropical trees, *Palaquium gutta* (earlier *Dichopsis guttata*) being the best.

RUBBER TREE (Hevea brasiliensis), *at one time the world's most important source of rubber. Its use in car tyres led to a tremendous demand for the tree.*

GUTTA-PERCHA (Palaquium gutta) *yields a rubber-like substance resistant to water and at one time widely used to insulate deep-sea telegraph cables.*

YELLOW CINCHONA (Cinchona calisaya) *has bark used in the preparation of quinine and widely used to combat malaria throughout the world.*

UNDER *the name Coca, the leaves of* Erythroxylum coca *(seen here being harvested) have long been used by the Indians of Peru and Bolivia as a nervous stimulant, hunger depressant and to enable long periods of work to be endured without fatigue. Nowaday cocaine, an important medicine, is extracted from them.*

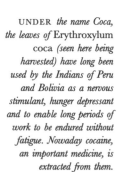

COFFEE (Coffea arabica) *is one of the world's most popular drinks. The commercial cultivation of coffee shrubs creates work for many people.*

AFRICAN OIL PALM (Elaeis guineensis) *has fruits that are a source of oil and glycerine, which was used in hospitals in the 1840s to treat skin diseases.*

PAPER MULBERRY (Broussonetia papyrifera) *has bark that was used in China to make paper and cloth. Sometimes the bark was used also to make rope.*

- Beverages: Tea, coffee (page 41) and cocoa (page 43) are well known and the staple drinks of many countries.
- Drugs: At one stage, plants provided the only drugs man knew, several being derived from shrubs and trees. The best known is the South American Fever Bark Tree (*Cinchona calisaya*), which provided quinine that helped to control the much feared malaria.
- Oils and waxes: These had many uses, including lighting, mixing with paints, as vegetable oils, for candles, soap production and lubricants for industrial machinery. Several palms provided some of these.
- Paper: Many trees have been used to create paper, including the Paper Mulberry (*Broussonetia papyrifera*) and *Yucca brevifolia* (see page 27).
- Cork: At one time, the Cork Oak (*Quercus suber*) was widely used for stoppers in bottles, floats for nets and in the construction of lifeboats. The waste materials were useful in the garden and were frequently used in window-boxes and growing orchids.
- Fibres: These are many and varied and include several palms.

Plantain

PLANTAIN (Musa paradisica) *has stems used experimentally during the late nineteenth century in paper-making, while a flour formed from the fruit is an excellent invalid food.*

COCONUT PALM (Cocos nucifera) *is a multi-purpose palm, producing fibres, coconut oil, food for livestock, thatching materials and wood.*

Coconut Palm

INTERNATIONAL SURVEY

THE GALAXY of shrubs and trees available from nurseries and garden centres is impressively wide. However, in recent years commercial pressures on nurseries have made it necessary for them to concentrate on the more popular species and varieties. Nevertheless, many specialists keep a wider range of plants than those normally offered for sale. Additionally, collections of specific types of plants are grown in collections to ensure they will not be lost.

The range of shrubs and trees normally grown within specific countries varies widely, usually according to the climate. For example, most shrubs and trees from temperate regions thrive in Britain, but even some of these are not fully hardy in all regions. In North America, however, the range of climates is so wide that shrubs from all over the world can

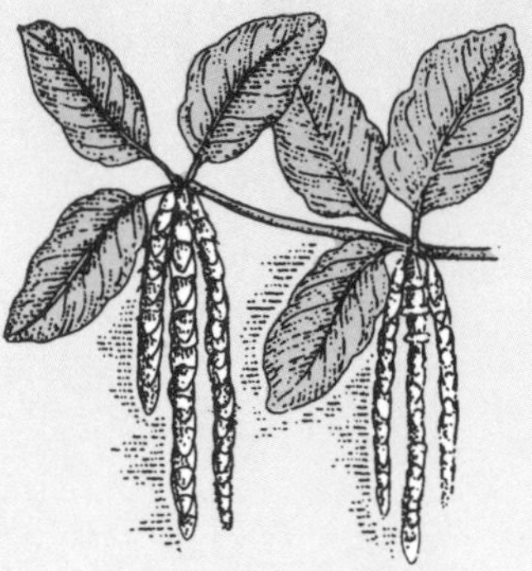

THE CATKIN-FACTOR

The North American Silk Tassle Bush (Garrya elliptica) *is famed for its grey-green catkins up to 23cm/9in long. It is an especially useful shrub, bringing colour to gardens during late winter and early spring. It is ideal as a wall shrub.*

CISTUS LADANIFER *(Gum Cistus) is an early summer-flowering evergreen shrub, native to south-west Europe and North Africa. The 6cm/2½in-wide white flowers have yellow centres and chocolate blotches.*

BUDDLEIA DAVIDII *(Butterfly Bush) is well known for its large, pyramidal heads of fragrant, lilac-purple flowers. There are many varieties, but the original species is native to Central and Western China.*

HYDRANGEA MACROPHYLLA *is deciduous and creates large flower heads during late summer on rounded shrubs. These are native to China and Japan and vary in colour from pink to blue.*

SHRUB OR TREE

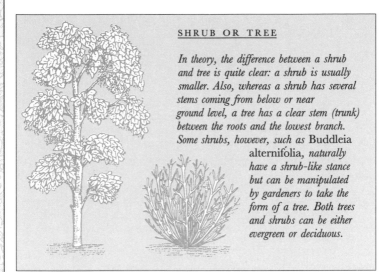

In theory, the difference between a shrub and tree is quite clear: a shrub is usually smaller. Also, whereas a shrub has several stems coming from below or near ground level, a tree has a clear stem (trunk) between the roots and the lowest branch. Some shrubs, however, such as Buddleia alternifolia, *naturally have a shrub-like stance but can be manipulated by gardeners to take the form of a tree. Both trees and shrubs can be either evergreen or deciduous.*

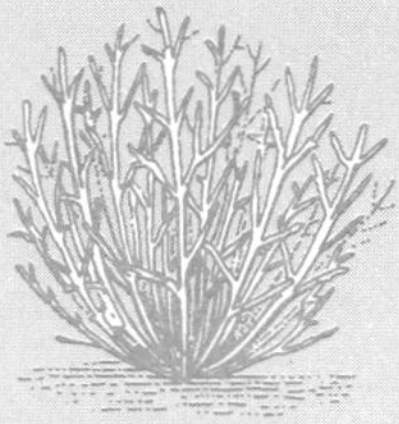

be grown: hardier ones in the north and tender ones from tropical and subtropical regions in the south – especially southern California. Indeed, many plants newly discovered in Southern Africa and subtropical parts of Australia were introduced into wider cultivation through places with compatible climates, such as California. It was also quicker to take antipodean plants California.

This book reveals a wealth of shrubs and trees that will enrich your garden with flowers throughout the year. Many of these are scented and therefore of additional value in gardens. There is also a rich kaleidoscope of shrubs, trees and conifers primarily grown for their attractive leaves; some evergreen and variegated, others with rich colours in autumn.

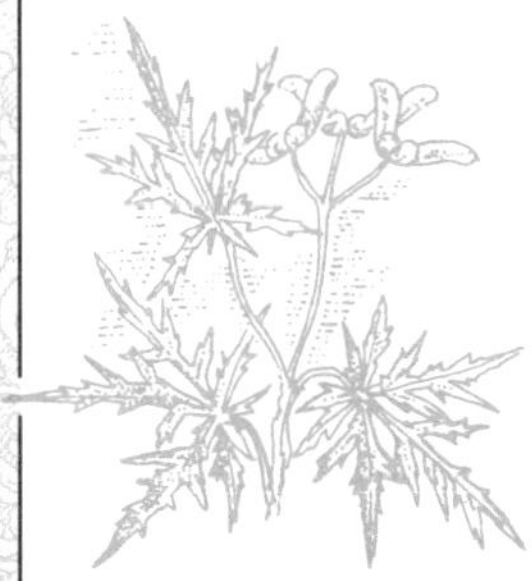

ACER PALMATUM *'Dissectum' is deciduous and forms a low, rounded bush with finely-cut, light green leaves. 'Dissectum Atropurpureum' is especially attractive, with beautiful bronze-red leaves.*

COTONEASTER HORIZONTALIS *'Variegatus' is a deciduous shrub with small, cream-white variegated leaves. It is slower growing than the normal and widely grown, all-green type.*

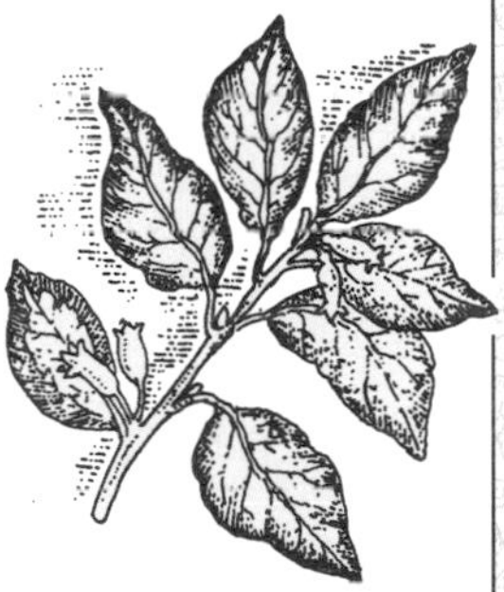

ELAEAGNUS PUNGENS *'Maculata' is an evergreen shrub with leathery, glossy-green leaves splashed in gold. The species is native to Japan. The form 'Variegata' has leaves elegantly edged in creamy-yellow.*

BUYING SHRUBS AND TREES

As MUCH care and thought is needed when buying garden plants as for any item in the home. Indeed, as shrubs and trees often outlive many household items – as well as perhaps dominating gardens for several decades – their selection needs much more careful thought.

Always buy shrubs and trees from reputable sources, as you not only want to be assured the plant is healthy, but that it is the variety you want. Send away for catalogues from well-known nurseries, as well as visiting local garden centres. And do not be unduly influenced by prices: high prices do not invariably mean better plants. Have a general look at the nursery or garden centre: if it is neglected and radiates little pride, this may be reflected in the quality of plants. And if in doubt about plants, talk to the manager to gain a further opinion. Inferior shrubs seldom recover to develop into satisfactory healthy plants.

WHAT TO LOOK FOR

Always inspect plants before buying them: if they are bought through the mail, check them when received and advise the supplier soon after if you are not satisfied.

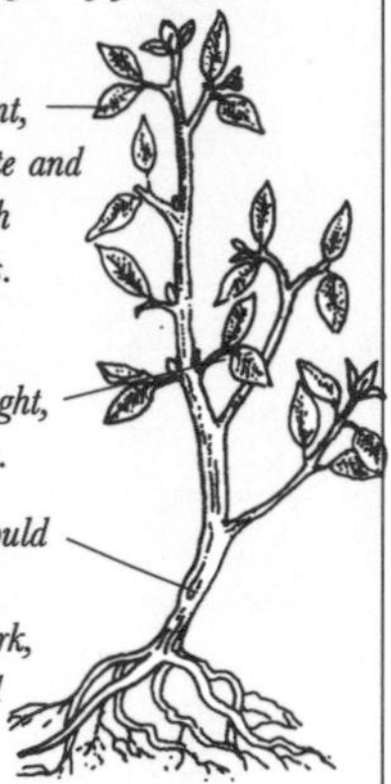

Leaves, if present, must be complete and not infested with pests or diseases.

Stems must be strong and straight, without damage.

Main stems should be completely covered with bark, and not gnawed by animals.

Bare-rooted plants should have roots well spaced out and not clustered at one side.

BALLED *plants are mainly conifers or small evergreen shrubs with hessian tightly wrapped around the root-ball. They are mainly sold during late summer and early autumn, or in spring.*

BARE-ROOTED *plants are deciduous shrubs and trees that have been dug up during their dormant period (late autumn to late winter), wrapped and despatched to customers for planting.*

CONTAINER-GROWN *shrubs and trees are either evergreen or deciduous, and can be planted throughout the year. These are sold mainly by garden centres, direct to gardeners.*

EARLY NURSERIES

Perhaps the first assurance that good, healthy plants would be offered for sale by nurserymen was in the seventeenth century, when in 1605 James I of England (James VI of Scotland) granted a charter to the Company of Gardeners which prevented the sale of 'dead and corrupt plants, seeds and stockes, and trees'.

Monastic gardens were probably the first source of seeds and plants in Europe. However, ornamental gardens in Persia certainly long pre-date the Christian era and their influence spread to Europe, possibly through Turkey, in about the middle of the fourteenth century. Earlier the Romans had been instrumental in spreading southern European plants throughout their empire.

AMERICAN NURSERIES

The earliest nurseries in North America were established by Robert Prince on Long Island in 1737, and slightly later by John Bartram in Philadelphia. Both were centres for the import of European plants, as well as the export of native ones. And both nurseries published extensive catalogues of trees, shrubs and herbaceous plants.

Incidentally, during the Revolutionary War (1793–1802), shipments of plants from Prince's Nursery to the Empress Joséphine in France were allowed to travel unharmed, in much the same way that the English nurseryman John Kennedy was allowed to travel regularly between London and France during the Napoleonic Wars (1805–1815) to advise Joséphine about her garden at Malmaison, just outside Paris. Joséphine also bought many plants from Kennedy's nursery, at a cost of £2,600 in 1802 alone.

WHERE TO BUY...

Shrubs and trees can be bought from several sources.

- Garden centres *mainly sell container-grown plants and therefore it is essential to visit them in a car, although some centres offer a delivery service within a limited area. From late autumn to late winter they may also sell bare-rooted shrubs, mainly roses.*
- Nurseries *offer bare-rooted as well as container-grown shrubs and trees. The container-grown ones – evergreen and deciduous – are available throughout the year, bare-rooted ones in winter and they are usually delivered by carriers. Balled evergreens are sent out in late summer and early autumn, as well as spring.*

- High street garden shops *offer a limited but popular range of container-grown plants, as well as bare-rooted shrubs, trees and roses from autumn to late winter.*

- Mail order nurseries *offer bare-rooted deciduous trees and shrubs, as well as balled ever greens. Specialist tree and shrub nurseries issue catalogues and it is wise to order the plants early. They are delivered by carriers.*

PREPARING AND PLANNING A SHRUB BORDER

MANY trees and shrubs are selected for specific places, perhaps to create focal points or to hide unattractive features. But they can also be used to form borders, when they are planted on their own or perhaps with underplantings of some small bulbs. Alternatively, they can be used in mixed plantings, where they jostle with herbaceous plants. Another choice is a floriferous winter garden or a scented border. But whatever the feature, it does need planning to ensure that colours do not clash, small shrubs are not hidden, or the balance between 'foliage' and 'flowering' shrubs is satisfactory.

Sketch out the garden's shape and size on graph paper, then draw in the borders and shrubs. When it looks right, try to visualize it on the ground by laying a hosepipe or thick rope to simulate the border's edge. View the area from all angles, as well as from upstairs rooms before finally deciding on the design.

HEIGHTS AND SPREADS

When planning a border, knowing the height and spread of each shrub or tree after a few years is essential. Therefore, throughout this book, heights and spreads of shrubs are given for a period of ten to fifteen years after being planted in good soil, an ideal position and a suitable climate.

Improve soil prior to planting by installing drainage, thorough cultivation and addition of decomposed organic material. Later, mulching and keeping the soil moist also helps. Unfortunately, it is more difficult to provide ideal positions when the area is windswept and exceptionally cold. In these areas, long-term planning includes planting windbreaks and hedges to reduce the wind's speed.

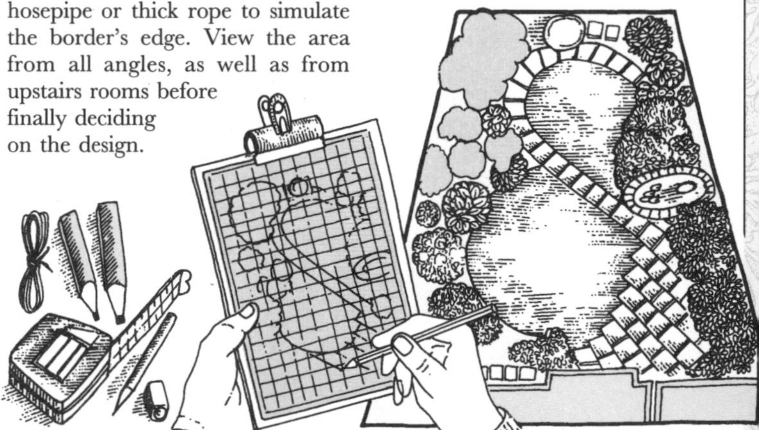

1. WHEN *shrubs and trees are planted into existing gardens, their selection is relatively easy. But for bare-site areas detailed planning is essential.*

2. SKETCH *the site's shape on graph paper, marking in fixed points such as fences and the house. Mark the paths and draw in borders. Then add shrubs and trees.*

3. TRANSFER *the plan to the garden. Slight modification may be necessary, so first outline the shape of the beds by using a long hose-pipe or rope.*

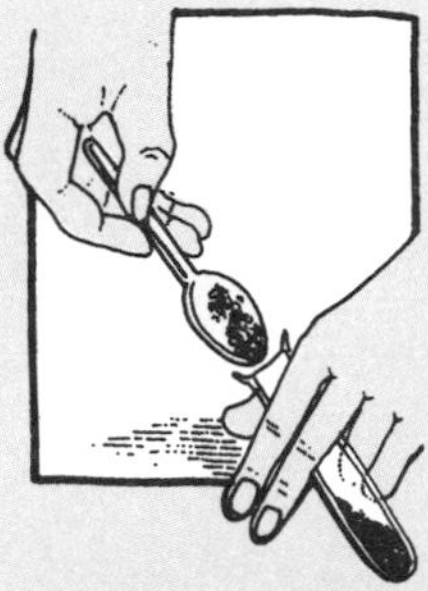

ASSESS *soil acidity by using a simple soil-testing kit: a sample is mixed with water, an indicator fluid added and the result compared with a colour chart to indicate the acidity. Alternatively, use a soil pH meter.*

MAKING SOIL LESS ACID

The amount of lime needed to reduce soil acidity (raising the pH) depends on the form in which it is applied and type of soil. As a guide, the following amounts of lime will decrease acidity by about 1 pH. First, however, check the soil with a pH soil-testing kit (left).

Soil	*Hydrated lime*	*Ground limestone*
Clay	*610g/sq m (18oz/sq yd)*	*815g/sq m (24oz/sq yd)*
Loam	*405g/sq m (12oz/sq yd)*	*545g/sq m (16oz/sq yd)*
Sand	*205g/sq m (6oz/sq yd)*	*270g/sq m (8oz/sq yd)*

SCENTED GARDENS

These are a special delight, and although climbers smothering arches with rich scents and colours are frequently thought to be the epitome of a scented garden, fragrant shrubs alongside a path are just as desirable.

It is possible to have scented shrubs in flower throughout the year, but winter is when they are especially appreciated. Ensure they are planted relatively close to a path, so that there is no temptation to tread on borders when trying to smell their fragrance. Incidentally, if elderly people are likely to use the path, make sure it is firm. For blind people ensure thorny roses are not nearby, and form paths with gravel edgings so that the sound, when walked on, indicates the edges. A range of sweetly-scented shrubs is detailed on pages 44 and 45. Create scented gardens in wind-sheltered positions and with a garden bench nearby, so that the fragrances can be appreciated at leisure.

CHLOROSIS

Acid-loving shrubs and trees in chalky soils often become chlorotic, causing leaves to whiten and bleach.

Chlorosis occurs when iron is 'locked up'. Adding ordinary iron to the soil does not help, because the high pH makes it unavailable to plants. To overcome this, apply chelated iron (sold as Sequestrene). Two or three applications a year should keep plants healthy.

Magnesium may also be deficient and is sometimes included in chelated products. Alternatively, apply Epsom salts (magnesium sulphate) as a foliar feed. Dissolve 3g in 1 litre (1/2oz in 1gal) of water. First, test this on a few plants.

PLANTING A CONTAINER-GROWN SHRUB

REMOVING from one house to another is invariably traumatic and fraught with problems, even for the most resilient person: being transferred from its nursery position to a place in a garden can be just as major for a shrub, tree or conifer.

In earlier times, the only choice between the types of plants to plant was 'bare-rooted' or 'balled'. Deciduous trees and shrubs were invariably sold as bare-rooted plants for planting during their dormant seasons (late autumn to late winter). Evergreens – and especially conifers – were sold as balled plants. These plants had been dug up and their roots (and soil) tightly wrapped in hessian. Planting time for these is during late summer and early autumn, or in spring when the soil has warmed up after winter.

Nowadays, a wide range of shrubs and trees is sold as container-grown plants. These are deciduous or evergreen trees and shrubs, as well as conifers, and can be planted at any time when the weather allows and the soil is not frozen or excessively wet.

CONTAINER-GROWN PLANTS
These have revolutionized gardening and enabled the modern fever for instant gardens to be satisfied.

Buy container-grown plants only from reputable nurseries: occasionally, plants in containers are offered for sale that until a few weeks earlier had been growing in nurserybeds, and therefore are not fully established in the container. When planting these, soil falls away from the roots and you are left with a plant which only pretends to be container grown. Ideally, the plant should have roots that fill – but not over-fill – the container, holding the compost in a firm ball.

1. THE *first step when planting a container-grown shrub or tree is to ensure the compost is moist. The day before planting, water the compost. It may be necessary to do this twice if exceptionally dry. Do not plant it if the ground is frozen or excessively wet, or the weather very cold.*

2. DIG *out a hole, wide and deep enough to accommodate the root-ball. Fork over the base, then firm and leave a slight mound. Place the plant in the hole and remove the container. The top of the soil ball should be slightly lower than the surrounding soil; this allows for subsequent soil settlement.*

3. GENTLY *firm friable soil in layers around the root-ball, taking care not to disturb its position and to push it sideways. Use the heel of your shoe to firm it evenly. When complete, thoroughly but gently water the soil to enable small particles to settle closely around the roots.*

1. UNTIL *the introduction of container-grown plants, most evergreen shrubs were sold 'balled': that is, the root-ball wrapped in hessian. They are still occasionally sold in this state. Take care not to knock the root-ball, as this dislodges its soil.*

2. THE *day before planting, thoroughly water the root-ball. Leave the hessian in place and dip the complete root-ball in a bucket of water until air bubbles cease to rise. Allow all water to drain away before planting the shrub or conifer.*

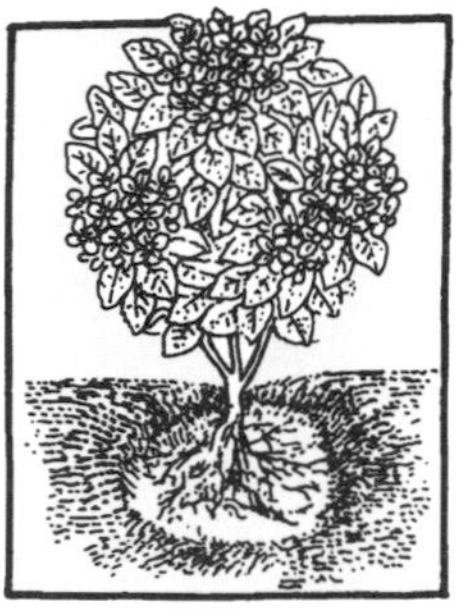

3. DIG *a hole large enough to accommodate the roots. Fork over its base, then firm to leave a slight mound. Place the roots on top and carefully remove the hessian. Tease out constricted roots and firm friable soil in layers around them.*

RAPID ESTABLISHMENT

After planting a shrub or tree, rapid establishment is essential, for several reasons:

- To anchor it in the soil and to prevent wind rocking it and loosening the roots. For this reason, use strong stakes to secure trees (see page 19).
- To enable roots to absorb quickly water and chemicals from the soil, thereby initiating growth processes. Water at this stage is especially important to replenish that lost by transpiration through the leaves. This is a continuous process that keeps leaves and stems cool. It also plays a role in the absorbtion of water from the soil, and its distribution throughout the plant.

Establishment is encouraged by watering the soil around trees and shrubs, then covering with a 7.5cm/3in mulch (layer of decomposed organic material). Additionally, preventing cold winds blowing on plants reduces transpiration (right).

WIND PROTECTION

Cold winter and spring winds damage newly-planted conifers and evergreen shrubs. Form a temporary screen of hessian on the windward side. Straw or hay sandwiched between two layers of wire-netting is another method – it can be formed into a U-shape and secured to the ground with strong stakes. Do not completely enclose plants, as a circulation of air is needed around their leaves and stems. In summer, newly-planted container-grown plants may also need protection from hot winds.

PLANTING A BARE-ROOTED SHRUB OR TREE

THESE are deciduous and planted during their dormant period, from late autumn to late winter, when free from leaves. They are usually ordered from nurseries and delivered by carriers, sometime during winter. If poor weather prevents them being planted immediately, dig a trench in a sheltered part of your garden and cover their roots with soil (see opposite page). However, if the soil is not frozen or excessively wet, and the delay is only for a few days, place them in a cool, dry shed or cellar. Loosen the wrappings to enable air to circulate around the stems.

PREPARATION FOR PLANTING

Remove all packing material and inspect the roots and branches. Cut off damaged roots and trim the ends off, particularly long ones. The roots should be relatively straight and spaced out around the trunk's base. Indeed, unless container-grown trees are in exceptionally large containers it is far better to buy them as bare-rooted types. A walk around many garden centres soon reveals large trees with their roots confined to containers often less than 30cm/12in wide. Trees with twisted roots never recover so that the plant is securely anchored by the roots to the soil.

Also, check the branches and use sharp secateurs to cut off damaged ones, leaving the remaining ones spaced out. If the roots are dry, stand them in a tub of water overnight before planting.

PLANTING AND STAKING

Planting is described and illustrated below, and the range of stakes on page 19. Whatever the method of staking, choose strong stakes – preferably of chestnut, oak, ash or spruce – long enough to allow at least 38cm/15in to be driven into the soil, with the stake's top just below the lowest branch.

Vertical stakes are inserted after the hole has been dug but before

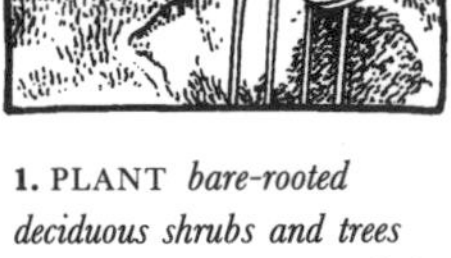

1. PLANT *bare-rooted deciduous shrubs and trees during their dormant period, from late autumn to late winter and whenever the soil is neither frozen nor too wet. Dig out a hole. Place the soil on a piece of sacking.*

2. FORK *over the hole's base and form a small mound. Position the plant, spread out its roots and use a straight board to check it is slightly deeper than before. The old level is indicated by a dark mark on the stem.*

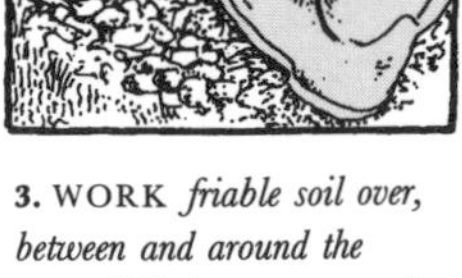

3. WORK *friable soil over, between and around the roots. Lift the stem up and down several times to enable friable soil to run between the roots. Replace friable topsoil in thin layers and firm it with your heel.*

1. SOMETIMES, *bare-rooted shrubs and trees arrive when either the soil is frozen or too wet. Also, you may not have the time to plant them immediately. Dig a trench 30cm/12in deep.*

2. CREATE *a small slope at one edge of the trench. Place the roots in the base and stems on the slope. Space them evenly and take care not to put them in one congested heap.*

3. SPREAD *soil over them and gently firm. Plants can be left like this for several weeks, but at the first opportunity plant them. Keep the soil moist to prevent roots drying.*

the tree is placed in position. If put in afterwards, the tree's roots may be damaged. Oblique stakes and H-types are put in afterwards, but because they extend out from the trunk may later impede grass cutting. The H-type is often used as a remedial support for standard trees if an earlier one has decayed. Also, if a tree is expected eventually to be self-supporting – such as large oaks and elms – it is easily removed later.

During the first few months after using a tree tie to secure a trunk to a stake, check it regularly to ensure the trunk's girth is not being restricted. Also, ensure that soil settlement has not caused the tree tie to strangle the trunk.

Because bare-rooted trees and shrubs are planted in winter, frost may later lift the soil. Therefore, in spring, re-firm the soil. At the same time, adjust the tree tie.

When a tree is planted in a lawn, do not replace turves close to the trunk as this will deprive the plant of both nitrogen and moisture. After a few years, the branches spread and bare soil is not so noticeable. If the tree is deciduous, plant some small spring-flowering bulbs underneath.

METHODS OF STAKING

Securing trunks of newly planted trees to stakes is essential to prevent roots being rocked. There are three basic methods:

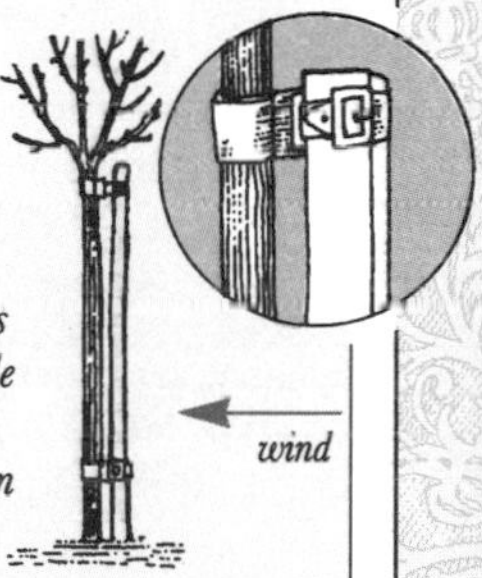

- *Vertical stakes are inserted while trees are planted and positioned on the windward side of the trunk. Its top must be just below the lowest branch.*

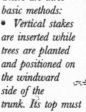

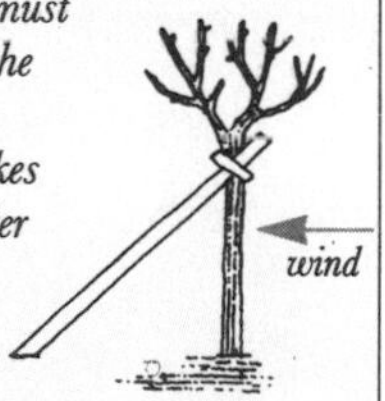

- *Oblique stakes are inserted after planting and best used for bushes or half-standards. The stake's top must face into the wind.*

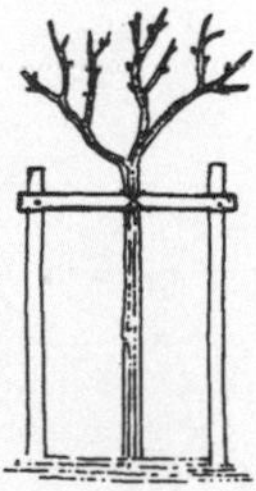

- *H-stakes are inserted after a tree has been planted and often used as a remedial measure.*

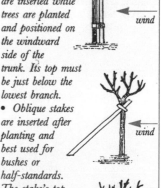

PLANTING A HEDGE

ONCE planted, a hedge might remain part of a garden for thirty or more years. Both its selection and planting therefore need care. A range of hedges primarily grown for their foliage is described and illustrated on pages 46 and 47, and flowering ones on pages 48 and 49. In addition, several of the trees and shrubs recommended on pages 54 and 55 for use in coastal areas can also be used as shelter belts and hedges where salt-spray is a problem.

CHOICE OF PLANTS

Hedges are created from several types of plants, which influences the times they are planted:

- Balled plants: usually evergreen shrubs and conifers; planted in late summer and early autumn, or in spring when the soil is warm.
- Bare-rooted plants: planted from late autumn to late winter.
- Container-grown plants: planted at any time when the soil and weather allow. Fuller details on pages 16 to 19.

PREPARING THE AREA

Prepare the planting position a few months before setting plants in the ground, using a spade to dig about 30cm/12in deep and a garden fork to break up the trench's base. If a single row of hedging plants is to be planted, prepare an area 30cm/12in wide. However, when planting a double, staggered row, prepare an area 15–18in/38–45cm wide.

Ensure all weeds are removed and fork in generous amounts of well-decayed compost. If the area is very wet, form a ridge and raise the soil level 15–30cm/6–12in, to a width of 60cm/2ft.

PLANTING THE HEDGE

When setting plants in a single row, use the spacings indicated on pages 45 to 49. However, for hedges formed of two rows (with individual plants staggered) space the plants about one-third of the suggested spacings further apart in the rows, with a similar distance between them.

HEDGES *grown for their attractive foliage can be evergreen, with green or variegated leaves throughout the year, or deciduous, with a chance of richly-coloured leaves in autumn. (See pages 46 and 47.)*

HEDGES *primarily grown for their flowers create dominant features, less formal than those grown for their attractive leaves. (See pages 48 and 49.)*

1. THOROUGH *soil preparation is just as essential for hedges as when planting shrubs and trees. Dig out a deep, wide trench, forking over the base and adding compost.*

2. POSITION *each plant so that it is slightly deeper than before (to allow for soil settlement) and spread friable soil around and over its roots. Ensure the plants are upright.*

3. FIRM *the soil by treading along the row. Loose planting leaves air pockets around the roots and retards establishment. It also encourages soil to become dry very quickly.*

Firm planting is essential, as well as spreading out the plant's roots.

Young plants will need to be watered until they are fully established, especially if the weather is dry immediately after they are planted. In such circumstances, it is more difficult to establish large plants than small ones.

Regular dressings of general fertilizers are essential in spring during a hedge's early years, especially if growth is slow and the soil sandy and poor.

It is essential to prune all hedging plants – except conifers – soon after they are planted. This encourages the development of shoots low down on plants, creating bushy growth from the hedge's base to its top.

Where hedges are planted along a boundary, ensure the plants are positioned at least half the expected width of the hedge in from the edge of your property. If planted directly on the boundary line, the hedge will intrude on the neighbouring property. Some neighbours will not mind this, but there is a risk that others will cut off shoots and leaves protruding on their side and may return them to you.

WALLS, FENCES AND HEDGES

If you live in a city, then the first choice of a barrier to separate your garden from a neighbour's is probably a brick wall or, at least, a high boarded fence. However, walls are expensive and time-consuming to construct and more likely than hedges to be blown over during high winds. Also, hedges are living parts of gardens and better able to harmonize with their surroundings.

Fences have a softer texture and outline than brick walls, but even these need clothing with climbers or wall-shrubs.

Hedges create less wind turbulence than walls and fences as they filter wind rather than creating a barrier that generates buffeting, plant-damaging currents.

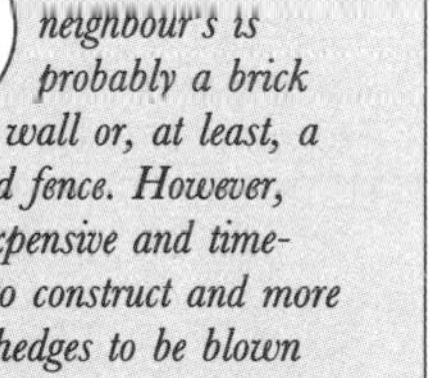

LOOKING AFTER TREES AND SHRUBS

APART from pruning (see pages 24 to 27) trees and shrubs need relatively little attention. However, there are a few tasks from which they benefit:

- Watering: Young, newly planted trees and shrubs must be regularly watered until well established. Thoroughly soak the soil, rather than just dampening the surface, which does very little good.
- Mulching: Young, newly planted shrubs and trees especially benefit from a 7.5cm/3in-thick layer of decomposed compost placed around them. First, remove all weeds and water the soil. Mulches are best applied in spring.
- Dead-heading: Immediately flowers fade, snap off the flower heads. This directs the plant's endeavours away from seed production.
- Water-shoots: Use a sharp saw to cut them off close to the trunk while still young. Pare the surface smooth with a sharp knife.
- Transplanting: Young trees and shrubs are relatively easy to move and plant (see pages 16 to 19), but mature ones are difficult. Evergreen types are best moved in late summer or early autumn, or in spring but after the soil has become warm. Deciduous types are transplanted when dormant.

Moving excessively large trees is best tackled in stages: the first year digging a trench around half the root-ball and refilling with peat and topsoil to encourage the development of fibrous roots; the second year completing the trench; and during the next season, digging up and moving.

In home gardens, few large trees are transplanted; shrubs are more likely to be moved and these can usually be dug up and replanted during the same season.

COVERING *the soil around a shrub or tree with a 7.5cm/3in-thick layer of well-decayed compost reduces moisture loss from the soil, as well as preventing the growth of annual weeds. Thoroughly water the soil before adding the mulch.*

REMOVE *faded flowers from shrubs such as large-flowered rhododendrons to prevent the formation of seeds and to direct the plant's endeavours into growth. Do not leave the dead heads on the ground, as they can look very untidy.*

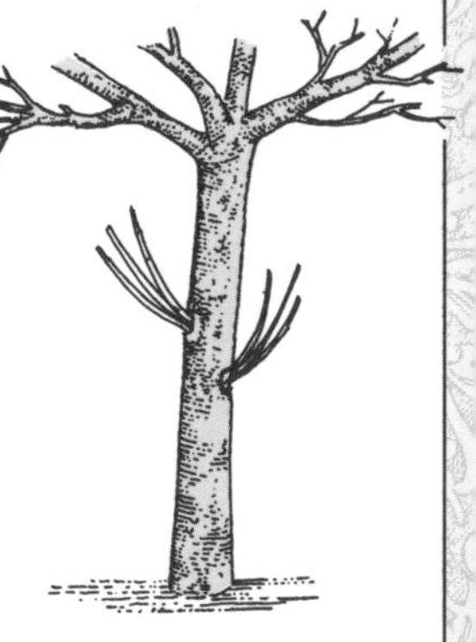

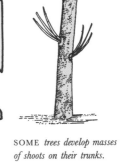

SOME *trees develop masses of shoots on their trunks. These must be removed by using a sharp saw to cut them back to the trunk. Then, use a sharp knife to smooth over any raised parts. This also prevents the formation of more shoots.*

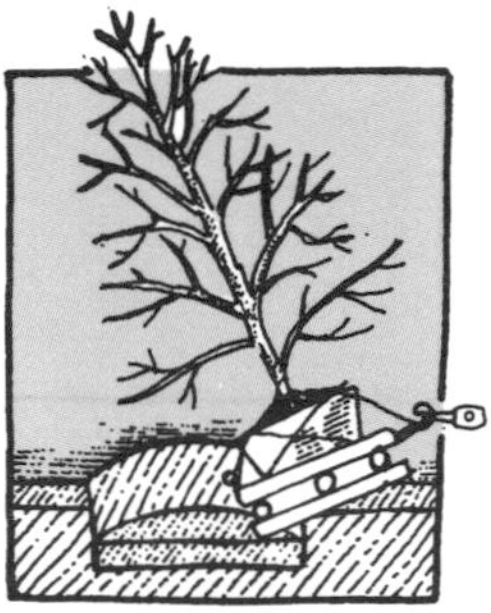

1. MOVE *established trees by digging around and underneath the soil ball. Wrap in hessian. Sandwich rollers between boards, place the soil ball on top and pull out of the hole.*

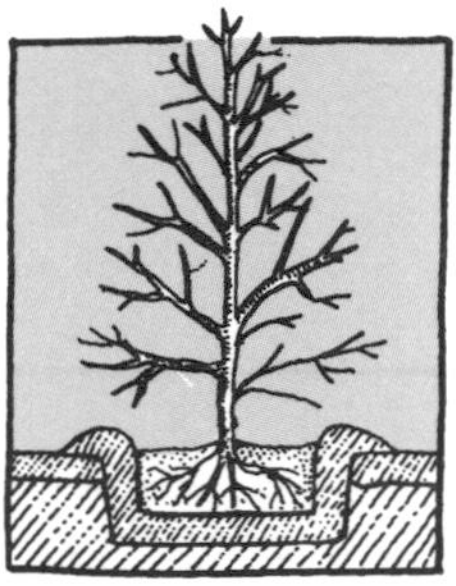

2. PLACE *the soil ball gently in a hole and spread out the roots. Pack and firm a mixture of peat and friable soil in layers over them. The peat will help in the retention of water.*

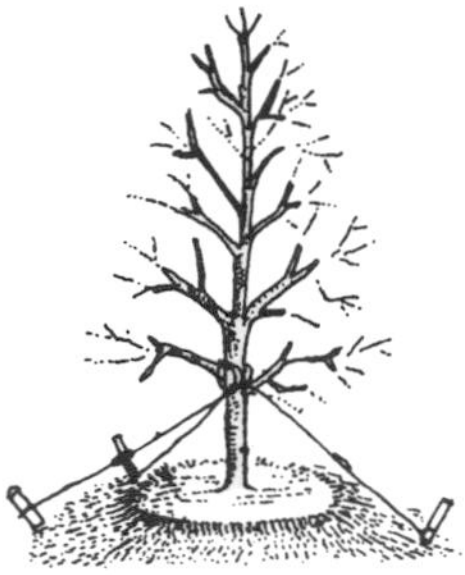

3. FIRMLY *stake the tree from at least three positions. Use loops of hose-pipe around the trunk, then guy ropes. In spring, cut back some branches to reduce loss of water from the leaf area.*

MOVING ESTABLISHED TREES

DURING *medieval times, trees were frequently moved while in full leaf.*

Large, established trees and shrubs have been moved for several thousand years. The Egyptians carried trees in wicker baskets suspended from poles borne by slaves. The Greek philosopher Theophrastus, writer and botanist, in about 300 BC *detailed the art of moving large trees; while the Romans knew the advantages of cutting back shoots and branches to reduce water loss.*

In the 1600s, the English diarist and gardener, John Evelyn, suggested an ingenious way to transplant mature trees: dig a large trench around the subject, undermining the root-ball. In winter, fill the trench with water which, when the temperature fell, would freeze and enable the root-ball to be removed without breaking.

In the seventeenth century, André le Nôtre's skills, when transplanting established trees to create 'instant' gardens at Versailles, were an inspiration to other gardeners. In the 1700s the English landscape designer Lancelot 'Capability' Brown designed a tree-transplanting apparatus formed of a stout pole fixed to an axle and two large wheels.

During the 1800s, the British landscape gardener William Barron became famous for moving very large trees. In 1880 he moved a gigantic, thousand-year-old yew in a churchyard about 54m/60yds to prevent its branches damaging the church.

MOVING *a large magnolia from Bordeaux to Paris in 1857.*

PRUNING DECIDUOUS SHRUBS

SOME deciduous shrubs need regular pruning to encourage the yearly development of flowers, while others require either none or very little. Shrubs that grow in temperate climates can be divided into three main flowering periods, which in turn influences the way they are pruned.

WINTER-FLOWERING SHRUBS

These are the easiest of all shrubs to prune, as usually they need little attention other than cutting out damaged, crossing or diseased shoots in spring. Always use sharp secateurs and cut back the shoots close to their bases. Do not leave small snags, which as well as looking unsightly, encourage the presence of diseases as they slowly decay and wither.

Because shoots are not drastically cut back each year, winter-flowering shrubs appear to grow slowly. But during their early years it is essential to ensure shoots do not cross one another and that the shrub develops an open centre and attractive shape.

Deciduous winter-flowering shrubs include the Chinese Witch Hazel *(Hamamelis mollis)*, Japanese Witch Hazel *(H. japonica)*, Ozark Witch Hazel *(H. vernalis)*, the richly scented Winter Sweet *(Chimonanthus praecox)* and the Cornelian Cherry *(Cornus mas)*.

Before

Before

Before

After

After

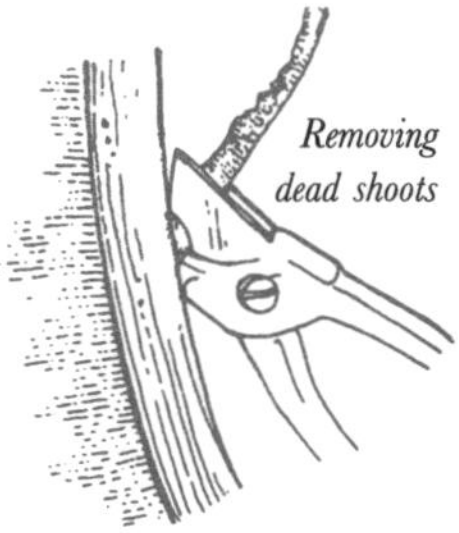

FORSYTHIA *swamps gardens with yellow flowers in spring. But to create this wealth of colour, cut out all old, damaged and diseased shoots when the flowers fade.*

THE *Butterfly Bush* (Buddleia davidii) *flowers in mid and late summer, but is not pruned until early in the following year. Cut back to encourage fresh shoots.*

THE *Chinese Witch Hazel* (Hamamelis mollis) *flowers in winter and needs very little pruning, just cut out crossing, diseased and damaged shoots.*

SPRING AND EARLY SUMMER-FLOWERING SHRUBS

These include some of the brightest and richly-flowered garden shrubs. They bloom on shoots produced during the previous year, from when the shrub finished flowering to the onset of cold weather in autumn.

These shrubs include Golden Bells (forsythia), Mock Orange (philadelphus), weigela (earlier known as diervilla) and Flowering Currants (ribes).

They are pruned immediately the flowers fade: cut out shoots that produced flowers, and thin out the shrub to enable light to enter, which is essential to encourage shoots to ripen before the onset of cold weather in autumn and winter. Also, remove crossing and diseased shoots, as well as those that are thin and spindly.

While pruning, check that the shrub's shape is balanced and not lop-sided. On mature shrubs, it may occasionally be necessary to cut out several large shoots at their bases to encourage regeneration at base level.

LATE SUMMER-FLOWERING SHRUBS

These enrich late summer and autumn with colour, their activities inevitably being curtailed by the onset of cold weather later in autumn.

They are pruned in spring, rather than after their flowers fade. This is because if they were pruned immediately after the flowers fade, it would encourage the development of young shoots that subsequently would be killed by frost. Therefore, by leaving pruning until the following year, in late winter or early spring (depending on the severity of weather in your area) young shoots that subsequently develop are ensured a safe life.

Well-known late summer-flowering deciduous shrubs include the Butterfly Bush *(Buddleia davidii)*, *Ceanothus* 'Gloire de Versailles' and Tamarisk *(Tamarix pentandra)*, with its wispy, smoke-like, deep rose-red flowers borne on slender, lax and spreading branches.

STEMS, LEAVES AND FLOWERS

Although most deciduous shrubs are grown for their flowers, others are primarily planted to create a feast of colourful stems. There is a wide range to choose from and some are detailed on page 59 as plants for boggy soils.

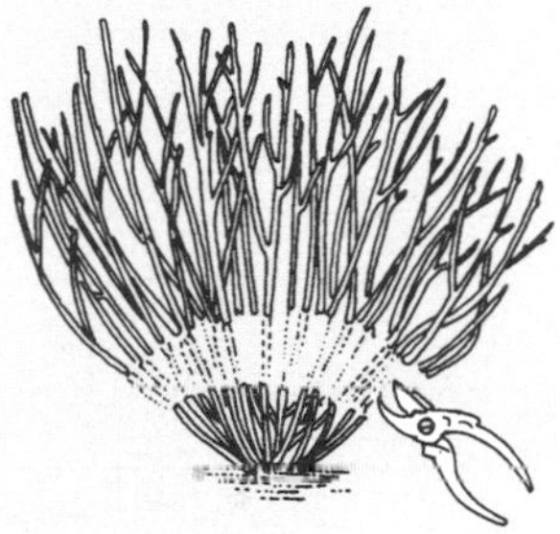

Cut down the stems in spring.

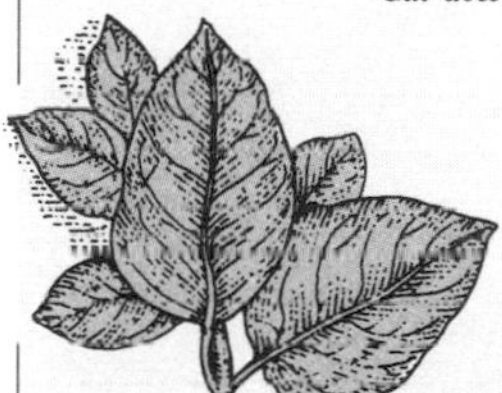

Many shrubs are grown for their colourful leaves (see pages 36, 37, 40 and 41).

There are flowering shrubs for all seasons (see pages 28 to 35).

PRUNING EVERGREEN SHRUBS

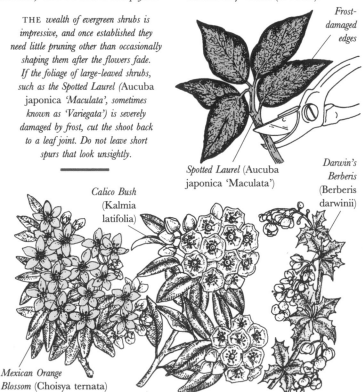

THESE are continually clothed in leaves, although throughout the year they fall off and fresh ones appear. Established evergreen shrubs need little pruning, other than cutting out weak, diseased and straggly shoots in spring. Frost-damaged shoots and leaves may also need to be removed. In cold areas, this task is left until early summer to prevent fresh shoots being damaged by severe, late frosts. Never prune them in winter.

If an evergreen shrub flowers in spring, delay pruning until the flowers have faded. Examples of this are Darwin's Berberis *(Berberis darwinii)* and *Berberis* x *stenophylla*.

TALL EVERGREENS WITH BARE BASES

Major surgery is needed when evergreens become tall, with bare bases. As soon as growth begins in spring, severe pruning can begin, but remember that the further back into old wood evergreens are cut, the more difficult it is for them to develop fresh shoots. Popular evergreen shrubs that respond to drastic pruning include Bay Laurel *(Laurus nobilis)*, Box *(Buxus sempervirens)*, Common Laurel *(Prunus laurocerasus)*, Daisy Bush *(Olearia* x *haastii)*, phyllyreas, Portugal Laurel *(Prunus lusitanica)*, many rhododendrons and Strawberry Trees (arbutus).

THE *wealth of evergreen shrubs is impressive, and once established they need little pruning other than occasionally shaping them after the flowers fade. If the foliage of large-leaved shrubs, such as the Spotted Laurel (*Aucuba japonica *'Maculata', sometimes known as 'Variegata') is severely damaged by frost, cut the shoot back to a leaf joint. Do not leave short spurs that look unsightly.*

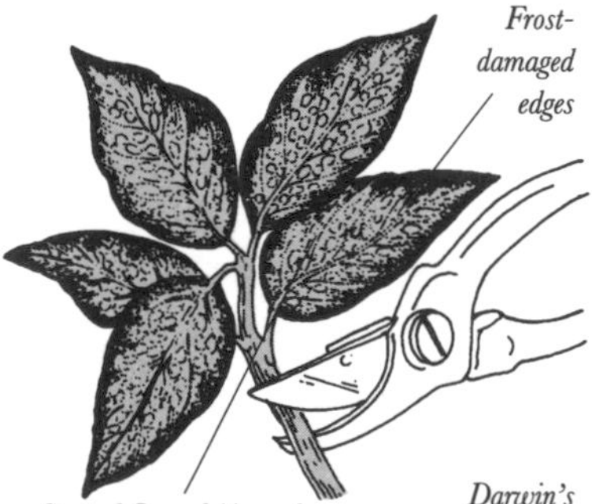

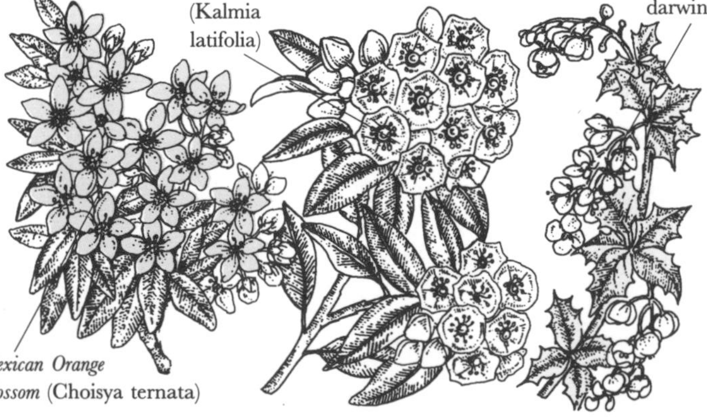

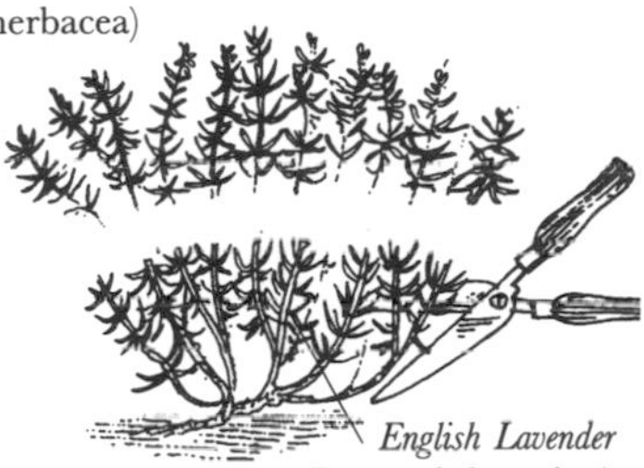

ERICAS *and callunas are ideal for creating massed colour as well as smothering soil and preventing the growth of weeds. Pruning them is simple: use hedging shears to lightly trim off dead flowers. On callunas and summer-flowering ericas, trim in late winter or spring. Winter and spring-flowering types are pruned after the flowers fade. Lavender (left) is also trimmed with shears, but in late summer.*

WHEN TRANSPLANTING EVERGREEN SHRUBS

Occasionally it is desirable to move an evergreen shrub from one place to another. This is relatively easy with small shrubs, but even then only those with a mat of fibrous roots are likely to survive. Tackle this task in late spring, when the soil is warming up, but before the weather becomes excessively hot.

To make this job easier and with a greater chance of success, cut the shrub's branches back by one-third to a half. Clearly, do not decimate the shrub, and cut back to sideshoots in a manner that creates a neat, balanced outline.

Keep as much soil as possible around the roots, and after replanting, regularly mist-spray the leaves for several weeks. Also, protect from drying winds (page 17).

SIGNPOSTS, PAPER AND NAPPIES!

Yuccas, native to North America, are distinctive evergreen shrubs with stiff, sword like leaves. One of the best known yuccas is the Joshua Tree (Yucca brevifolia) *which grows in Nevada, California and Arizona. It is thought to have been given this name in the belief that its leaves pointed only one way and would serve as a guide across the desert.*

Its thick stems have been converted into paper pulp and at one time were used to print the British Daily Telegraph. *In recent times, an extract from yuccas has been used in trials to deodorise babies' nappies.*

WINTER-FLOWERING SHRUBS AND TREES

DURING the cold, dull days of winter, flowering shrubs and trees are especially welcome. They range in size from ground-hugging types to those 1.8m/6ft or more high. Therefore, there are shrubs to fit all gardens, and several of them are featured here.

Because they bring colour to gardens when few other plants are flowering, position them where they can be seen easily; perhaps at the junctions of paths, sides of patios or as focal points a little way down a garden.

Winter-flowering shrubs need little pruning, other than removing dead, crossing or diseased shoots in spring, after the flowers fade.

Plant small bulbs under deciduous types to create extra colour in spring.

OTHER SHRUBS AND TREES

- Erica x darleyensis: *Early winter to late spring; range of varieties – white, pink or purple.*
- Erica lusitanica: *early winter to late spring; white.*
- Chimonanthus praecox: *early to mid-winter; yellow; spicy scent.*
- Hamamelis japonica: *late winter to early spring; yellow.*
- Lonicera fragrantissima: *early winter to early spring; creamy-white; fragrant.*
- Mahonia japonica: *early winter to early spring, lemon-yellow; lily-of-the-valley fragrance.*

CORNUS MAS

CORNELIAN CHERRY/ SORBET

Height: 2.4–3m /8–10ft

Spread: 1.8–2.4m / 6–8ft

Twiggy, deciduous shrub with dark leaves and small, yellow flowers from mid-winter to mid-spring. Edible, cherry-like, red fruits follow the flowers. In autumn, leaves assume reddish-purple shades before falling.

Slow-growing

DAPHNE MEZEREUM

FEBRUARY DAPHNE/ MEZEREON/ MEZEREUM

Height: 1.2–1.5m/ 4–5ft

Spread: 75cm–1.2m/ 2 1/2–4ft

Bushy, deciduous, somewhat erect shrub with scented, purplish-red flowers from late winter to mid-spring. These are followed by red, poisonous berries. Also, a white-flowered form.

Winter scent

DAPHNE ODORA

WINTER DAPHNE

Height: 1.2–1.5m/ 4–5ft

Spread: 1.2–1.5m/ 4–5ft

Bushy, slightly tender, evergreen shrub with shiny, mid-green leaves. Pale purple flowers appear in clustered heads from mid-winter to mid-spring. The form D. o. *'Aureomarginata' is hardier, with narrow creamy-white edges to the leaves.*

Delicious fragrance

ERICA HERBACEA

(E. CARNEA)

HEATHER/ SNOW HEATHER/ SPRING HEATHER

Height: 20–30cm/ 8–12in

Spread: 38–60cm/ 15–24in

Mound-forming, spreading, evergreen shrub with light green leaves, flowering from late autumn to late spring, depending on the variety. Wide colour range.

Easily grown

HAMAMELIS MOLLIS

CHINESE WITCH HAZEL

Height: 1.8–2.4m/ 6–8ft

Spread: 1.8–2.4m/ 6–8ft

Deciduous shrub or small tree with golden-yellow, spider-like, sweetly-scented flowers in early or mid-winter and continuing until early spring. Leaves turn yellow in autumn. Several forms: 'Pallida' has pale yellow flowers.

Slow growing

MAHONIA 'CHARITY'

HOLLY GRAPE

Height: 1.8–2.4m/ 6–8ft

Spread: 1.5–1.8m/ 5–6ft

Evergreen shrub with stiff, dark green, holly-like leaves and 23–30cm/ 9–12in-long spires of deep yellow flowers from late autumn to late winter. Ideal for planting in a wild garden, in moist soil and light, dappled shade.

Winter colour and fragrance

VIBURNUM TINUS

(LAURUSTINUS)

Height: 1.8–2.4m/ 6–8ft

Spread: 1.8–2.1m/ 6–7ft

Bushy, rounded, evergreen shrub with mid to deep green leaves and white, pink-budded flowers from late autumn to late spring. 'Eve Price' has a dense, compact habit and pink-tinged flowers that are carmine when in bud.

Easily grown

AMERICAN INFLUENCE

The Mahonia family was named in honour of the Irish-American horticulturalist Bernard McMahon, who lived from 1775 to 1816. He left Ireland for political reasons, in 1796 settled in Philadelphia and in 1806 published The American Gardener's Calendar, *which was still being reprinted more than fifty years later. He established a nursery and seed shop, which became a meeting point for botanists and nurserymen. Indeed, many seeds collected by plant hunters in North America were passed to him for germination, including those gathered by the Captains Merriwether Lewis and William Clark during their journey across North America during the first few years of the nineteenth century. Two well-known genera of plants named after these two men include Lewisia (herbaceous and evergreen semi-succulent perennials now grown in rock gardens) and Clarkia (a genus of hardy annuals).*

SPRING-FLOWERING SHRUBS AND TREES

TO MANY people, pink-flowered Japanese cherries are the epitome of spring, but there are other trees and shrubs to choose from. Dominant splashes of Gorse (ulex) are eye-catching on commons in spring, but also try planting the double-flowered form in your garden. Forsythia has a shorter flowering period, but is just as dominant when in bloom. Magnolias are also attractive, with large and spectacular flowers.

Some spring-flowering shrubs need regular pruning – but not all. Forsythia, for instance, needs to be pruned immediately its flowers fade, cutting out flowered wood; whereas Gorse needs no regular treatment, although leggy plants can be cut back in spring.

OTHER SHRUBS AND TREES

- Forsythia x intermedia: *early to mid-spring; golden-yellow. Many other forsythias flower during this season.*
- Pieris japonica: *early to mid-spring; white.*
- Prunus *'Kanzan': mid to late spring; double, purple-pink.*
- Prunus x yedoensis: *early and mid-spring; almond scented and bluish-white.*
- Ulex europaeus *'Plenus': mainly early to late spring; double and yellow.*
- Viburnum x burkwoodii: *early to late spring.*

AMELANCHIER LARMARCKII

(A. CANADENSIS)

JUNE BERRY/ SERVICEBERRY/ SHADBUSH/ SNOWY MESPILUS

Height: 2.4–3m/ 8–10ft

Spread: 2.4–3m/ 8–10ft

Large, rounded, deciduous, shrub with leaves turning soft red or yellow tints in autumn. Pure white flowers during mid-spring.

Ideal as a focal point

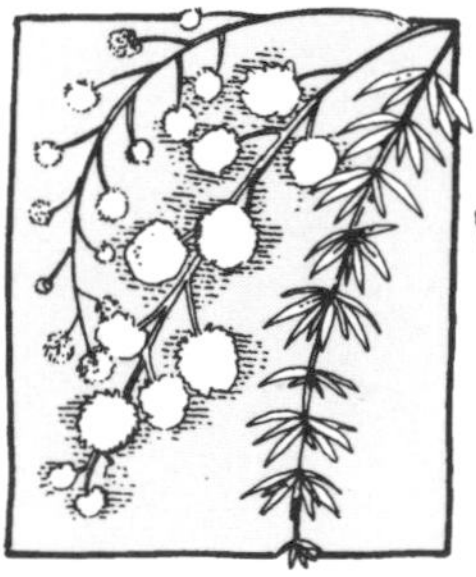

BERBERIS x STENOPHYLLA

Height: 1.5–1.8m/ 5–6ft

Spread: 1.8–2.4m/ 6–8ft

Widely grown, evergreen shrub with long, arching stems bearing small, dark green leaves and golden-yellow flowers during mid-spring. Round, purple berries appear in autumn, but they are rather sparse. It is often grown to form a wide, dense, arching hedge.

Easy to grow

CAMELLIA x WILLIAMSII

CAMELLIA

Height: 1.8–2.4m/ 6–8ft

Spread: 1.2–1.8m/ 4–6ft

Well-known, slightly tender evergreen shrub with glossy, dark green leaves. Flowers late winter to mid-spring, with many varieties in a range of colours, including white, pink and red, in single, semi-double and double forms.

Ideal in a wild garden

CHAENOMELES
x SUPERBA

CYDONIA/JAPONICA FLOWERING QUINCE/ JAPANESE QUINCE/

Height: 1.2–1.8m/ 4–6ft

Spread: 1.2–1.8m/ 4–6ft

A stiffly lax, deciduous shrub with clusters of flowers from early to late spring. Several varieties, in colours including red,crimson, vermilion, orange-scarlet and pink.

Hardy and slow growing

CYTISUS
x PRAECOX

WARMINSTER BROOM

Height: 1.5–1.8m/ 5–6ft

Spread: 1.5–1.8m/ 5–6ft

Tumbling, cascading, deciduous shrub with arching stems bearing grey-green leaves. During mid and late spring it bears fragrant, creamy-white flowers. 'Allgold' has rich, bright yellow flowers.

Easy to grow

KERRIA JAPONICA

JAPANESE ROSE/ JEW'S MALLOW

Height: 1.2–1.8m/ 4–6ft

Spread: 1.2–1.8m/ 4–6ft

Slender-stemmed, deciduous, rather lax shrub with bright green leaves and yellow-orange flowers during mid and late spring. 'Pleniflora' (widely known as Batchelor's Buttons) is popular and has double flowers.

Easy to grow

MAGNOLIA
STELLATA

(M. KOBUS STELLATA)

STAR MAGNOLIA

Height: 2.4–3m/ 8–10ft

Spread: 2.4–3.6m/ 8–12ft

Spreading, deciduous tree or large shrub with white, star-shaped, fragrant flowers during early and mid-spring. 'Rosea' has pink-flushed flowers, while the variety 'Water Lily' has larger flowers with more petals.

Slow growing

KEEPING KISSING IN FASHION

Gorse – also known as Furze and Whin – flowers mainly in spring. In some areas it continues in bloom intermittently through to late winter of the following year. This nearly year-around blooming encouraged the old saying:

'When Gorse is out of bloom,
Kissing is out of season'

For this reason, a sprig of Gorse was often put into bridal bouquets.

Mistletoe, a parasitic shrub that lives upon trees such as apples, is used to encourage kissing at Christmas. It was originally a wholly English custom but has spread to most countries settled by the English: any person found standing under a bunch of mistletoe at Christmas must now expect to be kissed.

Part of this early enthusiasm for kissing is said to derive from an early English custom of men and women freely kissing when meeting and parting, which continued until the early seventeenth century.

EARLY SUMMER-FLOWERING SHRUBS AND TREES

EARLY summer encourages even more shrubs to burst into flower, flooding gardens with colour. In large gardens, complete borders can be devoted to them, but they are just as attractive when planted close to paths, perhaps just around a corner where they create a surprise – especially when both colourful and scented. Mock Orange (philadelphus) is especially fragrant and always attracts attention.

A few of these shrubs, such as potentilla, flower from early to late summer, while others continue from late spring to early or mid-summer. The exact times of flowering are strongly influenced by the weather in your area; planting a shrub against a warm wall encourages early flowering.

OTHER SHRUBS

- Carpenteria californica: *early to mid-summer; white.*
- Deutzia *'Magician': early to mid-summer; mauve-pink edged in white. Also, 'Mont Rose' (pink).*
- Helianthemum nummularium: *early to mid-summer; range of varieties in colours including orange-yellow, yellow, copper, scarlet, pink and cream.*
- Philadelphus *Hybrids: early to mid-summer; mainly white.*
- Potentilla *Hybrids: early to late summer; range of colours.*
- Syringa vulgaris: *early summer; range of colours.*

BUDDLEIA GLOBOSA
ORANGE-BALL TREE
Height: 2.4–3.6m/8–12ft
Spread: 2.1–3m/7–10ft
A slightly tender evergreen shrub that during cold winters can lose some of its leaves. During late spring and early summer it develops clusters of scented, rounded, orange-yellow flowers at the ends of long, slightly lax stems.
Often damaged by frost

CISTUS 'SILVER PINK'
ROCK ROSE
Height: 60–90cm/2–3ft
Spread: 60–90cm/2–3ft
Low-growing evergreen shrub with thick-textured, dark green leaves and 7.5cm/3in-wide, clear pink flowers with yellow centres during early and into mid-summer. There are other hybrids, including C. *x* lusitanicus.
Ideal for small gardens

HEBE
'MIDSUMMER BEAUTY'
Height: 1–1.2m/3½–4ft
Spread: 1.2–1.5m/4–5ft
Bushy, evergreen shrub bearing light green leaves with reddish undersides. From early to late summer – sometimes into autumn – it bears long tassels of lavender-coloured flowers. Other hebes include 'Great Orme' (bright pink).
Easy to grow

KOLKWITZIA AMABILIS

BEAUTY BUSH

Height: 1.8–3m/3–10ft

Spread: 1.5–2.4m/5–8ft

Upright, but slightly drooping and spreading, deciduous shrub with stems covered in peeling, brown bark. During late spring and early summer it develops pink flowers with yellow throats. 'Pink Cloud' is popular, with clear pink flowers.

Spectacular shrub

PAEONIA SUFFRUTICOSA

(P. MOUTAN)

MOUTAN PAEONY/ TREE PAEONY

Height: 1.2–1.5m/4–5ft

Spread: 1.2–1.8m/4–6ft

Outstandingly attractive, slightly tender shrub with white, single flowers up to 15cm/5in across during early summer. Several forms, including 'Rock's Variety' (white with crimson blotches).

Damaged by frost

SENECIO 'SUNSHINE'

Height: 1.2–1.5m/4–5ft

Spread: 1.2–1.8m/4–6ft

Dome shaped, evergreen shrub bearing silvery-grey leaves with white, felted undersides. Yellow, daisy-like flowers appear in clustered heads during early and into mid-summer. The foliage is especially attractive when covered with frost or a light covering of snow.

Easy to grow

WEIGELA – *HYBRIDS (DIERVILLA)*

Height: 1.5–1.8m/5–6ft

Spread: 1.5–1.8m/5–6ft

Deciduous hybrids created by crossing Weigela florida with Asiatic species. Spectacular flowers during late spring and early summer. Varieties include 'Abel Carriere' (soft rose), 'Bristol Ruby' (rich ruby-red) and 'Avalanche' (vigorous and white).

Easy to grow

LONE-BUSHES IN IRELAND

Thorn trees have had historic significance as places of judicial assemblies in Britain since before the Romans arrived. They have also had important roles in Ireland, where solitary thorn trees were known as Lone Bushes. They were revered and believed to be trysting trees for 'the Little People'. It was said that these trees were ideal because of their appearance, often looking like 'miniature monarchs of the forest'. To cut down a Lone Bush was thought to bring ill luck and possibly death.

It was the custom for passing pilgrims to hang medals, crucifixes and rosary beads on these trees in acknowledgement of, and thanks for, cures obtained from them.

Thorn trees at crossroads had further significance because the partings of roads were considered meeting places of the spirits. It was also the custom for funeral processions to stop and place crosses on the branches before passing on to the cemetery.

LATE-SUMMER FLOWERING SHRUBS AND TREES

BY MID-SUMMER, gardens frequently reveal a surfeit of flowers, but there are many more exciting shrubs waiting to burst into bloom. Some may have been in bloom since mid-summer, while others reveal their glories solely in late summer and through to the frosts of autumn.

A few of these shrubs have a dominant size, while others are better suited to small gardens. Many, such as *Yucca gloriosa* and *Ceanothus* 'Gloire de Versailles', can be merged into 'mixed' borders to live cheek-by-jowl with herbaceous perennials (plants that die down to soil level in autumn). *Hydrangea macrophylla* is a well-known late-flowering shrub and includes the Hortensia (Mophead) and Lacecap types.

OTHER SHRUBS AND TREES

- Ceanothus *'Gloire de Versailles': early summer to early autumn; soft powder-blue.*
- Fuchsia magellanica: *mid-summer to autumn; crimson and purple.*
- Hydrangea macrophylla *(Hortensia and Lacecaps): mid to late summer; blue and pink.*
- Lavandula spica*: mid to late summer; pale grey-blue. 'Hidcote' is deep purple-blue.*
- Romneya coulteri*: mid to late summer; white.*
- Yucca gloriosa: *late summer to late autumn; creamy-white, tinged red.*

CARYOPTERIS x CLANDONENSIS

BLUEBEARD

Height: 60cm–1.2m/2–4ft

Spread: 60cm–1.2m/2–4ft

Hardy, deciduous shrubs with narrow, aromatic, grey-green leaves and upright stems bearing clusters of blue flowers during mid and late summer. Varieties include 'Arthur Simmonds' and 'Heavenly Blue'.

Easy to grow

ESCALLONIA – *VARIETIES*

Height: 1.5–2.1m/5–7ft

Spread: 1.5–2.1m/5–7ft

Rounded, bushy, evergreen shrub with flowers from early to late summer and even into early autumn. Varieties include 'Crimson Spire' (bright crimson), 'Donard Brilliance' (rose-red), 'Peach Blossom' (pink) and 'Pride of Donard' (bright rose).

Easy to grow

EUCRYPHIA x NYMANSENSIS

Height: 3–4.5m/10–15ft

Spread: 1.8–2.4m/6–8ft

Quick-growing evergreen tree with erect branches, shiny green leaves and cream flowers during mid and late summer. Other eucryphias include E. glutinosa, *which is slow growing and has white flowers with large, yellow centres.*

Plant in a wild garden

THE BAMBOO GARDEN

These are members of the grass family that bring many attractive qualities to gardens: they have attractive stems and leaves, create often near impenetrable screens and, even in gentle breezes, produce a continuous rustling. They like moisture-retentive soil that does not dry out during summer, and shelter from cold winds. And they grow well in sun or partial shade.

Transplanting them is best left until the soil has warmed up in early summer, and do not be surprised if during the first season the stems die back slightly or make little growth. No pruning is needed. They create a new and unusual dimension to gardens and once established need no attention.

Their range is wide and includes:

- Arundinaria japonica *(3–4.5m/10–15ft high): large, dark, glossy green leaves.*
- Arundinaria murieliae *(1.8–2.4m/6–8ft high): beautiful arching stems with narrow, bright green leaves.*
- Arundinaria nitida *(2.4–3m/8–10ft high): purple stems with light green leaves.*
- Arundinaria viridistriata *(1–1.5m/3½–5ft high): dark green leaves striped rich yellow.*
- Phyllostachys nigra *(2.4–3m/8–10ft high): Young stems mature to black after several seasons.*
- Sasa veitchii *(60cm–1.2m/2–4ft high): shiny, green leaves with straw-coloured edges in autumn.*

HIBISCUS SYRIACUS

ALTHAEA
Height: 1.8–2.4m/6–8ft
Spread: 1.5–1.8m/5–6ft
Hardy, deciduous shrubs with stiff stems and rich green leaves. From mid-summer to autumn it bears a succession of flowers in a wide colour range (depending on variety) including white, pink, red and purple.
Slightly tender

HYDRANGEA PANICULATA *'GRANDIFLORA'*

Height: 2.4–3.6m/8–12ft
Spread: 2.4–3.6m/8–12ft
Hardy, deciduous shrub with terminal clusters up to 30cm/12in long of white flowers, which age to pink, during mid and late summer. Hydrangea arborescens *is another late-flowering hydrangea, with large, dull white flowers.*
Vigorous growing

HYPERICUM *'Hidcote'*

(H. patulum *'HIDCOTE'*)
Height: 90cm–1.2m/3–4ft
Spread: 1.2–1.5m/4–5ft
A deciduous or semi-evergreen shrub with deep green leaves and a profusion of golden-yellow, saucer-like flowers from mid-summer to autumn. The smaller H. olympicum *is ideal for planting in sinks or large rock gardens.*
Easy to grow

COLOURED LEAVES

FLOWERS are attractive but invariably transient in their display. Coloured leaves, however, can be with you throughout the year if the plant is evergreen, or from spring to autumn when deciduous. And even the departure of deciduous leaves in autumn initiates bright colours. Trees and shrubs with bright autumn colours are detailed on pages 40 and 41.

Some of these shrubs are small and ideal for planting in mixed borders. Others are tall and dominant and better as focal points towards the end of a garden. They can even be used to create colour contrasts, with perhaps the rich purple leaves of *Cotinus coggygria* 'Foliis Purpureis' set against the soft, rich yellow leaves of *Robinia pseudoacacia* 'Frisia'.

OTHER SHRUBS AND TREES

- Acer negundo *'Variegatum': deciduous; pale green leaves irregularly edged in white.*
- Artemisia arborescens: *deciduous or semi-evergreen; silver-white.*
- Calluna vulgaris *'Gold Haze': evergreen; bright gold leaves.*
- Gleditsia triacanthos *'Sunburst': deciduous and spineless; bright yellow young leaves.*
- Griselinia littoralis *'Dixon's Cream': evergreen; apple green leaves splashed creamy-white.*
- Ruta graveolens *'Jackman's Blue': evergreen; glaucous blue.*

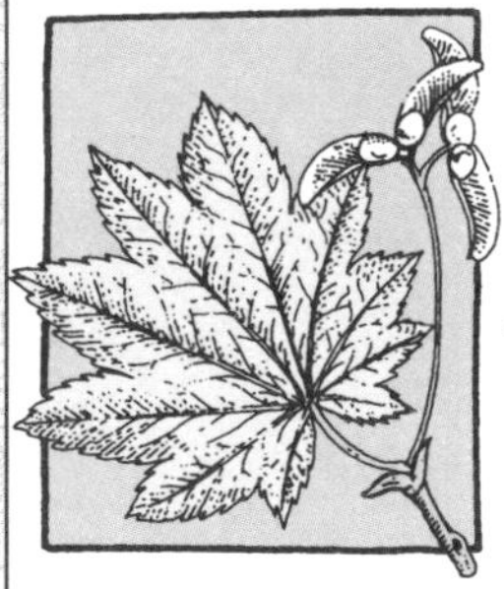

ACER JAPONICUM
'AUREUM'
Height: 3–4.5m/10–15ft
Spread: 2.4–3.6m/8–12ft
Hardy, deciduous tree with beautiful soft-yellow leaves that turn rich crimson in autumn. Other forms include 'Aconitifolium' (deeply lobed leaves that assume ruby-crimson tints in autumn) and 'Vitifolium' (crimson tints in autumn).
Slow growing

ACER PALMATUM
'ATROPURUREUM'
Height: 3–4.5m/10–15ft
Spread: 2.4–3m/8–10ft
Hardy, deciduous tree with brilliant purple leaves in summer, assuming rich crimson-purple shades in autumn. Also A. p. *'Dissectum Atropurpureum' (finely divided bronze-purple leaves) 'Dissectum' (soft green).*
Shelter from cold winds

CATALPA BIGNONIOIDES
'AUREA'
GOLDEN INDIAN BEAN TREE
Height: 3.6–4.5m/12–15ft
Spread: 3.6–4.5m/12–15ft
Hardy, deciduous tree with large, velvety, soft-yellow leaves. White, foxglove-like flowers, marked in yellow and purple, appear during mid-summer. These are followed by slender beans.
Slow growing

CORYLUS MAXIMA

'PURPUREA'

PURPLE-LEAF FILBERT/ HAZEL

Height: 2.4–3m/ 8–10ft

Spread: 2.4–3m/ 8–10ft

Deciduous shrub with large, rounded, rich-purple leaves. Other hazels include C. avellana *'Aurea' with soft yellow leaves and yellow catkins up to 6cm/ $2^{1}/_{2}$in long in late winter.*

Very hardy

COTINUS COGGYGRIA

'FOLIIS PURPUREIS'

Height: 3–3.6m/ 10–12ft

Spread: 2.4–3m/ 8–10ft

Also known as 'Notcutt's Variety', this hardy, deciduous shrub has foliage first crimson, later rich purple and with light red shades in autumn. Soft, wispy flowers cover the shrub in early and mid-summer.

Easy to grow

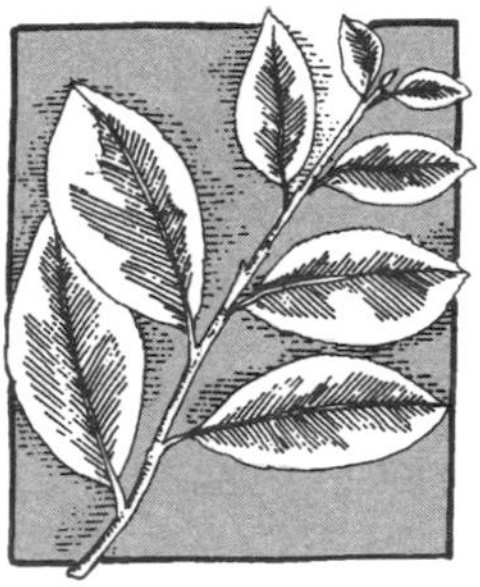

EUONYMUS JAPONICA

'OVATUS AUREUS'

Height: 1.2–1.5m/ 4–5ft

Spread: 1–1.2m/ $3^{1}/_{2}$–4ft

Hardy, evergreen shrub with mid-green leaves edged and suffused in creamy-yellow. It needs a sunny position for the leaves to retain their colour. There are many other variegated forms.

Slow growing and compact

PHILADELPHUS CORONARIUS

'AUREA'

GOLDEN-LEAVED MOCK ORANGE

Height: 1.8–2.4m/ 6–8ft

Spread: 1.5–1.8m/ 5–6ft

Dense, deciduous shrub with young, bright yellow leaves. In summer they often become greenish-yellow. Creamy-white, flowers during early and mid-summer.

Full or light shade

PSEUDOACACIA

'FRISIA'

COMMON ACACIA/ BLACK LOCUST/ FALSE ACACIA

Height: 6–7.5m/ 20–25ft

Spread: 3–4.5m/ 10–15ft

Hardy, deciduous tree with leaves first golden-yellow, later pale green. They are formed of small leaflets. Creamy-white fragrant flowers appear in early summer.

Plant as a focal point

SAMBUCUS RACEMOSA

'PLUMOSA AUREA'

GOLDEN ELDER

Height: 1.8–2.4m/ 6–8ft

Spread: 1.8–2.4m/ 6–8ft

Hardy, deciduous, bushy shrub with deeply divided, golden-yellow leaves. Yellow flowers appear during mid and late spring followed by scarlet berries during mid-summer.

Slow growing

COLOURED BARKS AND SHOOTS

TREES with coloured barks, as well as shrubs with attractive shoots, are especially welcome in winter and early spring, when often there is little colour about and leaves have not yet arrived on deciduous plants.

Some of these trees, such as the Paperbark Tree (*Acer griseum*) can be planted as specimens in lawns, while others look superb when grouped together and surrounded in spring by crocuses. Birches are especially attractive when used in this way; plant them so that low rays from the sun can glance on their trunks.

The Windmill Palm *(Trachycarpus fortunei)* needs a mild climate. Eventually it has a long, attractive trunk which enables planting close to a path.

OTHER SHRUBS AND TREES

- Acer griseum: *buff-coloured bark flakes to reveal light orange-brown underbark. Leaves colour in autumn.*
- Arbutus x andrachnoides: *peeling, cinnamon-red bark.*
- Betula ermanii: *peeling bark, orange-brown changing to creamy-white.*
- Betula jacquemontii: *white, peeling bark.*
- Betula utilis: *outstandingly attractive peeling bark, orange to brown or coppery-brown.*
- Cornus alba: *red stems.*
- Cornus alba *'Sibirica': bright crimson shoots.*

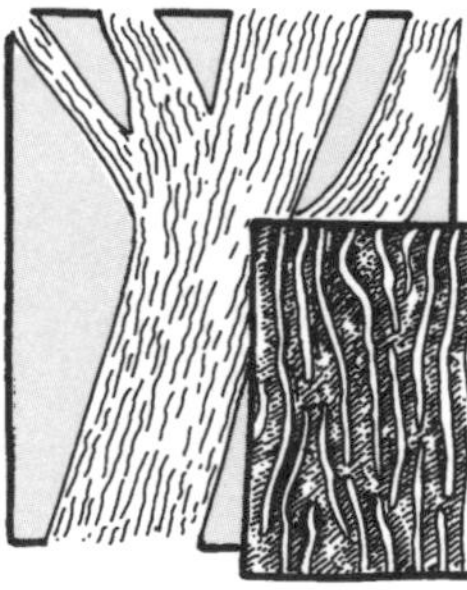

ACER DAVIDII

SNAKEBARK MAPLE

Height: 4.5–6m/15–20ft

Spread: 2.4–3m/8–10ft

Hardy, deciduous tree with grey bark lined in white. The form 'George Forrest' has spreading branches with dark green leaves that assume handsome tints in autumn. A. pensylvanicum *also has bark that is attractively striped in white.*

Plant in light shade

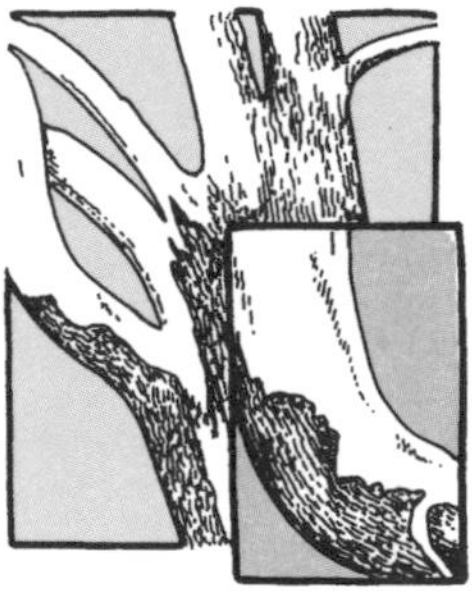

ARBUTUS ANDRACHNE

GRECIAN STRAWBERRY TREE

Height: 3–4.5m/10–15ft

Spread: 2.4–3m/8–10ft

Slightly tender, but becoming hardier, evergreen tree with peeling, cinnamon-red bark. White flowers in terminal clusters during early and mid-spring, followed by unusual orange-red, strawberry-like fruits.

Needs shelter

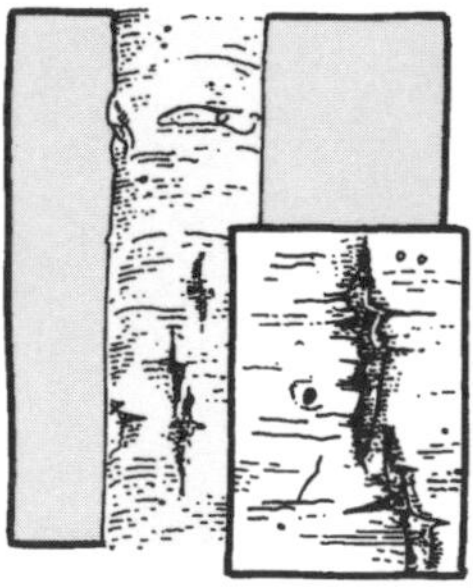

BETULA PAPYRIFERA

CANOE BIRCH/PAPER BIRCH/ WHITE BIRCH

Height: 4.5–6m/15–20ft

Spread: 3–3.6m/10–12ft

Beautiful, hardy, deciduous tree with gleaming white bark that peels in strips, especially on old trees. In autumn, the triangular, mid-green leaves assume attractive yellow shades.

Ideal specimen tree

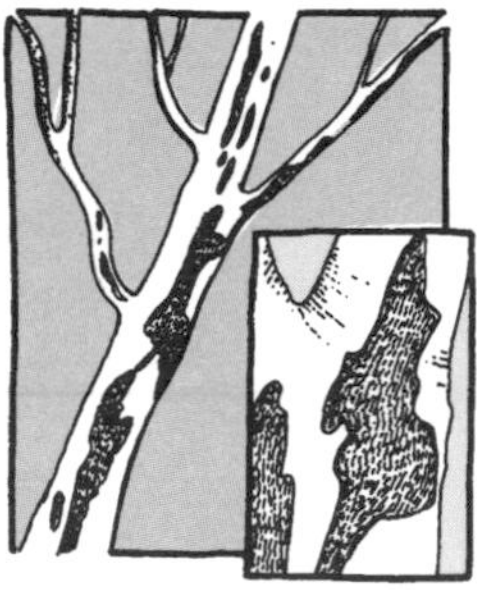

EUCALYPTUS NIPHOPHILA
ALPINE SNOW GUM/ SNOW GUM
Height: 6m/20ft
Spread: 4.5m/15ft
Hardy, wind-resistant, deciduous tree with outstandingly attractive bark. On young trees the bark is bluish-white. After four or five years, bark is shed annually, revealing pale cream underbark.
Fast growing

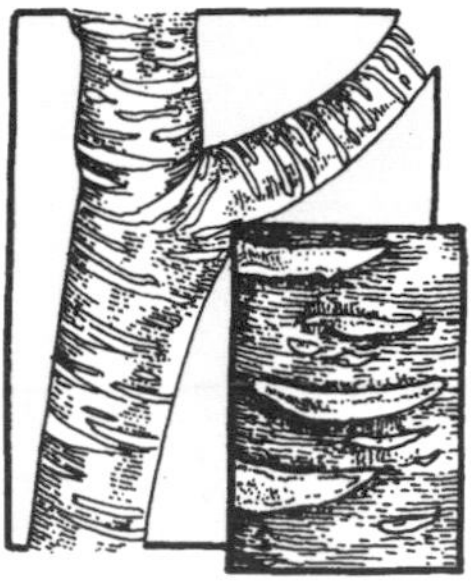

PRUNUS SERRULA
Height: 4.5–6m/15–20ft
Spread: 3.6–4.5m/12–15ft
Hardy, deciduous tree with spectacular bark peels in strips to reveal polished, mahogany-like, reddish-brown underbark. During mid-spring it develops small, white flowers, although it is the bark that is the main attraction. Many gardeners who grow this tree regularly polish the bark.
Slow growing

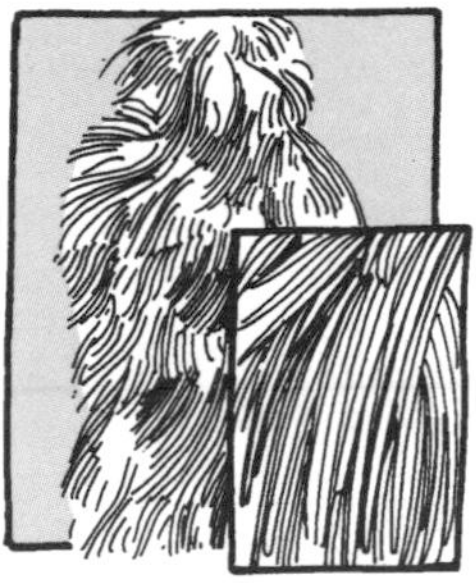

TRACHYCARPUS FORTUNEI (CHAMAEROPS EXCELSA)
CHUSAN PALM/FAN PALM/ WINDMILL PALM
Height: 1.8–3m/6–10ft
Spread: 1.8–2.4m/6–8ft
Beautiful palm, with large fans of mid-green, pleated leaves often 90cm/3ft across. The trunk becomes covered in dark fibres that create a wonderful feature.
Not fully hardy

THE LANGUAGE OF FLOWERS

About four hundred years ago it became fashionable in Constantinople (now Istanbul) for amorous thoughts to be expressed by passing flowers. Clearly, it was not a total language, but enough information was included for lovers to exchange thoughts. Certain flowers expressed specific information, while even the angle and way in which flowers were given and accepted had a meaning. As well as garden and wild flowers, shrubs and trees had a significant role. Here are a few of them:

ACACIA = Friendship
AMERICAN LINDEN = Matrimony
APPLE BLOSSOM = Preference
APRICOT = Ardour
ASH TREE = Grandeur
AZALEA = Temperance
BEECH TREE = Prosperity
BIRCH = Meekness
BROOM = Humility
CEDAR LEAF = I live for thee
CHERRY TREE (WHITE) = Deception
CHESTNUT TREE = Luxury
CYPRESS = Death/Mourning
FIR = Time
GUELDER ROSE = Winter/Age
HAWTHORN = Hope
HOLLY = Foresight
LABURNUM = Forsaken
LAUREL = Glory
LAVENDER = Distrust
MAGNOLIA = Love of nature
MYRTLE = Love
OLEANDER = Beware
PEACH BLOSSOM = I am your captive
ULEX = Humility
WITCH HAZEL = A spell

AUTUMN-COLOURED LEAVES

MANY deciduous shrubs and trees have leaves that assume rich tints of red and yellow in autumn before falling. In years when the weather is dry in autumn and a frost rapidly stops growth, the colours are richer than ever.

The Stag's Horn Sumach (*Rhus typhina*) is ideal in small gardens but many other autumn brighteners have a uniform, slightly clinical outline that makes them more suitable as focal points towards the bottom of a garden or perhaps framed in a lawn. These include the Swamp Cypress (*Taxodium distichum*) and the Sweet Gum (*Liquidambar styraciflua*). *Acer cappadocicum* has a more irregular shape and eventually creates a dominant feature. Position it towards the end of a garden.

OTHER SHRUBS AND TREES

- Cercidiphyllum japonicum: *red and yellow autumnal tints.*
- Enkianthus campanulatus: *brilliant red shades.*
- Ginkgo biloba: *bright gold in autumn.*
- Hamamelis mollis: *yellow leaves in autumn.*
- Liriodendron tulipifera: *tulip-shaped leaves become butter-yellow in autumn.*
- Malus tschonoskii: *rich red and yellow autumnal foliage.*
- Quercus rubra: *dull crimson then deep reddish-brown.*
- Taxodium distichum: *leaves bright red in autumn.*

ACER CAPPADOCICUM

MAPLE

Height: 5.4–6m/18–20ft

Spread: 3.6–4.5m/12–15ft

Hardy, deciduous tree, spreading with age. The five or seven-lobed dark green leaves become soft yellow in autumn. The form 'Aureum' has red foliage when young, becoming golden-yellow. 'Rubrum' turns gold.

Eventually large

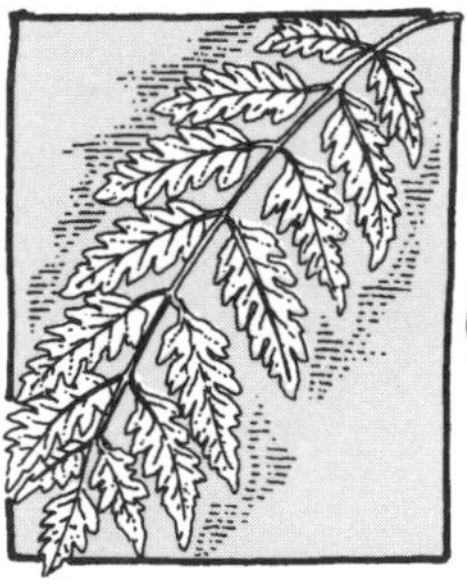

KOELREUTERIA PANICULATA

CHINA TREE/GOLDEN RAIN TREE/PRIDE OF INDIA

Height: 3–4.5m/10–15ft

Spread: 2.4–3m/8–10ft

Handsome, hardy, deciduous tree with large, mid-green leaves up to 35cm/14in long and formed of several leaflets. In autumn they assume yellow tints. Yellow flowers appear in mid-summer.

Eventually large

PARROTIA PERSICA

Height: 3–4.5m/10–15ft

Spread: 3–3.6m/10–12ft

Hardy, deciduous shrub or tree with rounded, mid-green leaves that in autumn develop crimson, gold and amber tints. Sometimes, these also include yellow. Additionally, the bark on old trees flakes in patches. Plant this tree in either light shade or full sun.

Slow growing

LIQUIDAMBAR STYRACIFLUA

BILSTED/ RED GUM/ SWEET GUM

Height: 5.4–6m/ 18–20ft
Spread: 2.4–3.6m/ 8–12ft
Hardy, pyramidal, deciduous tree with dark green, maple-like, lobed leaves that assume rich orange and scarlet shades in autumn. The form 'Lane Roberts' has black, crimson-red autumn colours.

Ideal on lawns

RHUS TYPHINA

STAG'S HORN SUMACH/ VELVET SUMACH

Height: 2.4–3.6m/ 8–12ft
Spread: 3–3.6m/ 10–12ft
Spreading, deciduous shrub with brown-felted stems and mid-green leaves formed of many leaflets that assume rich orange-red, purple and yellow tints in autumn. The form 'Laciniata' has deeply divided leaves.

Ideal for small gardens

ON THE COFFEE TRAIL

*'There's an awful lot of coffee in Brazil', goes the well-known song, but this world-famous drink originated many miles away, in Abyssinia, now Ethiopia. The date when the virtues of the coffee shrub (*Coffea arabica*) were discovered is uncertain: one story tells of a prior who, upon learning that his cattle sometimes browsed on this shrub and then bounded all night on the hills, became curious. He then tried the beans on his monks to prevent them sleeping at matins.*

Constantinople coffee shop

The drink spread through Egypt and Syria, reaching Constantinople in 1511, where in 1554 a coffee-shop was opened. Coffee later became a popular drink in Vienna and Germany. The first coffee-houses in England opened in Oxford in 1650 and a few years later in St. Michael's Alley in the City of London. The passion for coffee spread rapidly among the wits and beaux, and especially among traders who used coffee-houses as places to discuss commerce. Merchants and brokers engaged in the Russian trade congregated in a subscription room at the Baltic coffee-house, while the Chapter in Paternoster Row was the resort of booksellers. There was also The Jamaica for the West Indian trade, while Lloyd's, Robin's and The Jerusalem were for general traders.

North American licence

The first licence to sell coffee in North America was granted in 1670. The Blue Anchor Tavern was opened in Philadelphia in about 1684. Ye Crown Coffee House was opened in 1711 on Boston Pier by Jonathan Belcher, and later Fraunce's in New York joined the ranks.

The French traveller Thevenot took coffee to France in 1662, but it was Soleiman Aga, the Turkish Ambassador, who made it fashionable in Paris.

BERRIES AND FRUITS

THESE bring a further dimension to gardens and are especially welcome in autumn – many of them persist through to late winter. Botanically, berries are fleshy or succulent fruits and contain a number of seeds. To gardeners, the difference is usually of no matter, as both of them create attractive features. Birds, however, are usually more tempted by fruits than berries, which tend to be harder. Nevertheless, few berries escape the affection of birds, especially during long, cold winters.

Some plants do not produce berries until both male and female plants are present. Where this is necessary, one male plant will normally pollinate several females, so buy them in a ratio of three to five females to one male.

OTHER SHRUBS AND TREES

- Aucuba japonica: *bright scarlet berries on female plants.*
- Crataegus x prunifolia: *large, persistent, red fruits.*
- Daphne mezereum: *scarlet berries (but poisonous).*
- Hippophae rhamnoides: *masses of bright-orange berries.*
- Mahonia japonica: *bunches of blue-black berries.*
- Malus: *'Golden Hornet': bright yellow berries.*
- Malus: *'Red Sentinel': persistent, deep red fruits.*
- Viburnum opulus: *translucent red berries.*
- Viburnum davidii: *bright, turquoise berries.*

ARBUTUS UNEDO
CANE APPLES/ KILLARNEY STRAWBERRY TREE
Height: 3.6–5.4m/ 12–18ft
Spread: 3–4.5m/ 10–15ft
Evergreen shrub with white or pink, pitcher-shaped flowers from early autumn to early winter. These often appear at the same time as orange-red, strawberry-like fruits that resulted from the previous year's flowers.
Slightly tender

CALLICARPA BODINIERI GIRALDII
BEAUTY BERRY
Height: 1.2–1.5m/ 4–5ft
Spread: 1.5m/ 5ft
Deciduous, bushy shrub with pale green leaves that assume yellow and red tints in autumn. The lilac-coloured, late-summer flowers are followed by exceptionally attractive round, deep lilac to violet-blue berries.
Not fully hardy

COTONEASTER HORIZONTALIS
FISH-BONE COTONEASTER/ HERRINGBONE COTONEASTER
Height: 45–60cm/ 1 1/2–2ft
Spread: 1.5–1.8m/ 5–6ft
Hardy, deciduous shrub; spreads or grows upwards. Branches like fish-bones bear dark green leaves. Small, pink, early-summer flowers are followed by red berries.
Easy to grow

FOOD OF THE GODS

It was not without good reason that the Swedish botanist Carolus Linnaeus named the cocoa tree Theobrama cacao, *theobrama meaning 'food of the Gods'. Long before Christopher Columbus chanced upon the American continent, cocoa was prized as a drink in Peru and Mexico. Indeed, the name chocolate is derived from xocotlatl, a contraction of two Nahuatl words meaning fruit and water. Cocoa was introduced into Europe in 1502 when Christopher Columbus returned with the first beans. However, they failed to impress Queen Isabel la Catónica, who claimed that they could not compensate for his inability to find a route to the East Indies.*

The cocoa beans are borne in pods that resemble small rugby footballs. These ripen to orange, red and purple.

PERNETTYA MUCRONATA

Height: 75–90cm/ $2\frac{1}{2}$–3ft

Spread: 1.2–1.5m/ 4–5ft

Hardy, evergreen shrub with glossy, dark green leaves. Small, white flowers in early summer; clusters of berries in autumn, in colours including white, pink, rose, purple and red. The presence of both male and female plants are essential to produce a crop of berries.

Ideal for acid soils

PYRACANTHA

'WATERERI'

FIRETHORN

Height: 1.8–2.4m/ 6–8ft

Spread: 1.8–2.4m/ 6–8ft

Hardy, evergreen, dense and twiggy shrub with white flowers in early summer and bright red berries from autumn to late winter. Other species and varieties have orange-red, rich yellow and orange berries.

Easy to grow

SKIMMIA JAPONICA

Height: 90cm–1.2m/ 3–4ft

Spread: 1.2–1.5m/ 4–5ft

Hardy, evergreen, dense shrub with leathery, pale green leaves. Creamy-white, fragrant flowers in late spring and bright red berries in late summer on female plants. Male and female plants are needed to produce berries. There are several attractive forms.

Slow growing

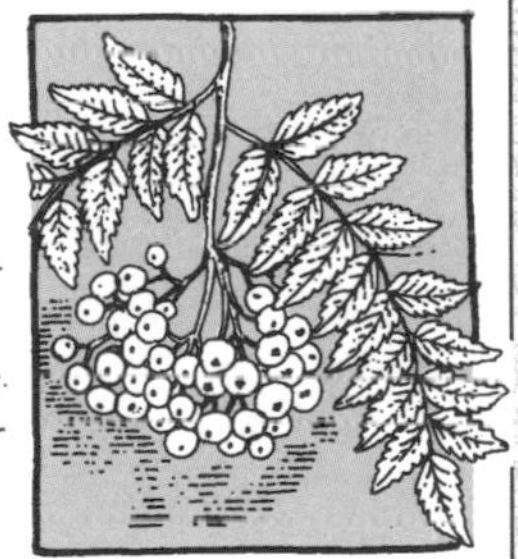

SORBUS

'JOSEPH ROCK'

Height: 4.5–5.4m/ 15–18ft

Spread: 2.4–3m/ 8–10ft

Hardy, deciduous tree with a compact but upright habit and green leaflets that assume orange-red shades in autumn. Cream-coloured flowers in late spring and creamy-yellow berries, maturing to amber, in autumn.

Easy to grow

SCENTED SHRUBS AND TREES

SOME gardens have a cold and unloved nature, but those rich in scents instantly create warmth and a general feeling of well-being. The range of scents is remarkably wide and apart from plants that enrich the air with sweetness there are those that are more original: Gorse (*Ulex europaeus*) is honey-scented, Mexican Orange Blossom (*Choisya ternata*) reveals an orange redolence, *Corylopsis pauciflora* has a bouquet that resembles cowslips, while *Magnolia sieboldii* presents a lemony bouquet. Many roses also have rich and varied scents.

Position these redolent shrubs and trees where their fragrances can be appreciated, and remember that wind-sheltered positions are the best choice.

OTHER SHRUBS AND TREES

- Buddleia davidii: *lilac-purple; mid-summer. Also, forms in white, violet-purple and blue.*
- Daphne odora *'Aureomarginata': pale purple; mid-winter to mid-spring.*
- Fothergilla monticola: *creamy-white; late spring; richly coloured leaves in autumn.*
- Hamamelis mollis: *golden-yellow; early winter to spring.*
- Laburnum x vossii: *yellow; early summer.*
- Lavandula spica: *pale grey-blue; mid to late summer.*
- Prunus padus: *almond-scented and white; late spring.*

CHIMONANTHUS PRAECOX (C. FRAGRANS)
WINTER SWEET
Height: 1.5–2.1m/5–7ft
Spread: 1.5–2.1m/5–7ft
Hardy, deciduous, bushy and twiggy shrub with cup-shaped, pale yellow, sweetly scented flowers from early to late winter. 'Grandiflorus' has deep yellow flowers.
Slow growing

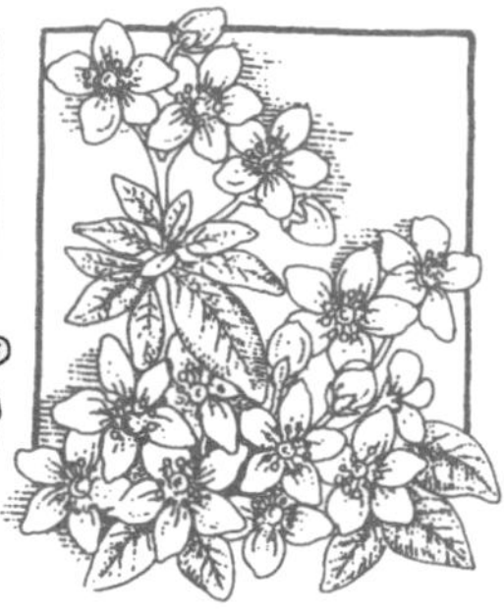

CHOISYA TERNATA
MEXICAN ORANGE BLOSSOM
Height: 1.5–1.8m/5–6ft
Spread: 1.5–2.1m/5–7ft
Rounded, densely leaved, evergreen shrub with dark green leaves that are aromatic when crushed. Sweetly scented white flowers in late spring and early summer. 'Sundance' is slower growing, smaller and with golden leaves. Ideal in tubs.
Slightly tender

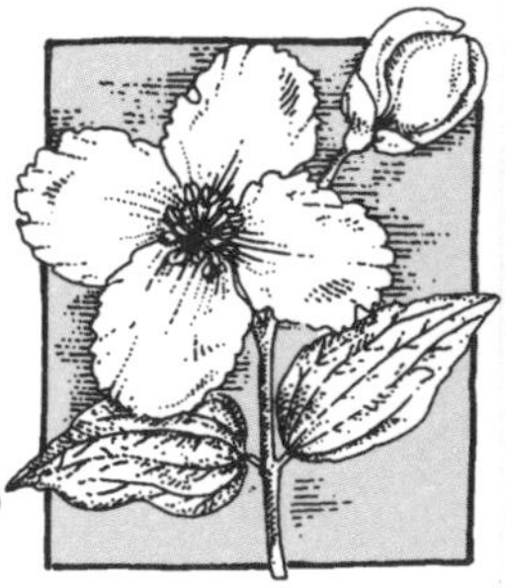

PHILADELPHUS
'BELLE ETOILE'
MOCK ORANGE
Height: 2.4–3m/8–10ft
Spread: 3–3.6m/10–12ft
Hardy, deciduous shrub; white flowers with maroon centres. Other varieties are 'Avalanche' (height 1.2–1.5m/4–5ft), 'Beauclerk' (1.8–2.4m/6–8ft) and 'Virginal' (2.4–2.7m/8–9ft).
Quick growing

ROSMARINUS OFFICINALIS
ROSEMARY
Height: 1.5–1.8m/ 5–6ft
Spread: 1.2–1.5m/ 4–5ft
Decorative, evergreen shrub with mid to dark green, slightly aromatic leaves. From mid-spring to late summer it bears mauve flowers. There are several forms, including 'Albus' (white or pale blue).
Spreads with age

SYRINGA VULGARIS
COMMON LILAC
Height: 2.4–3m/ 8–10ft
Spread: 2.1–2.7m/ 7–9ft
Hardy, deciduous shrub (can be grown as half and full standards) with fragrant, lilac-coloured flowers (single, semi-double and double forms). There are many superb forms, in colours including white, pink and lavender.
Slow growing

ULEX EUROPAEUS
'PLENUS'
FURZE/ GORSE/ WHIN
Height: 1.5–2.1m/ 5–7ft
Spread: 1.5–2.1m/ 5–7ft
Hardy, evergreen, spiny shrub with scale-like leaves and honey scented, double, golden-yellow flowers mainly from early to late spring but often through to late winter of the following year. Ideal in a country garden.
Slow growing

KING COTTON

King cotton transformed nations, creating great wealth and, initially, demanding a great labour force in the southern states of North America, formed mainly of slaves. The merits of cotton plants had been known for centuries – from Peru to China – but in the eighteenth century the sudden acceleration of technical developments in Britain and Europe made it possible to process raw materials at a much faster rate.

The development of any industry is not an even progression: rather a series of leap-frogs from resolving one limiting factor to the next. In 1733, John Kay, an English inventor, patented the flying shuttle, an automatic device which moved a shuttle across the loom. This speeded up weaving and increased the demand for spinning yarn. In 1764, James Hargreaves invented the spinning jenny which increased the production of yarn. Five years later, Richard Arkwright patented an improvement. The next advancement came in 1779 from Samuel Crompton and was called the spinning mule. At about the same time, the Scottish engineer, James Watt, developed steam power. And when in 1793 the American, Eli Whitney, invented the cotton gin, to remove the lint from the seeds, the stage was set for the rapid expansion of King Cotton.

Gossypium barbadense

FOLIAGE HEDGES

HEDGES are essential features in gardens, creating both privacy and beauty. Also, they are better than walls at providing shelter from cold, strong winds: solid screens create turbulence, while hedges gently filter strong gusts.

Hedges range in height from the diminutive Edging Box (*Buxus sempervirens* 'Suffruticosa') to the somewhat infamous hybrid conifer Leyland Cypress (X *Cupressocyparis leylandii*). Its growth rate is impressive: 3.6m/12ft in six years and 15m/50ft in fifteen. It is therefore better in large gardens, where it can be planted as a windbreak. The form 'Castewellan Gold' has golden-yellow foliage in summer.

Planting hedges is detailed on pages 20 and 21.

OTHER SHRUBS AND TREES

- Buxus sempervirens *'Suffruticosa': evergreen; plant 23cm/9in apart; low hedge.*
- Carpinus betulus: *deciduous; plant 45–60cm/1½–2ft apart; tall.*
- Chamaecyparis lawsoniana: *evergreen; conifer; plant 38–45cm/15–18in apart; tall.*
- *X* Cupressocyparis leylandii: *evergreen; conifer; plant 60–75cm/2–2½ft apart; fast-growing.*
- Ilex aquifolium: *evergreen; plant 45cm/1½ft apart, medium to tall.*

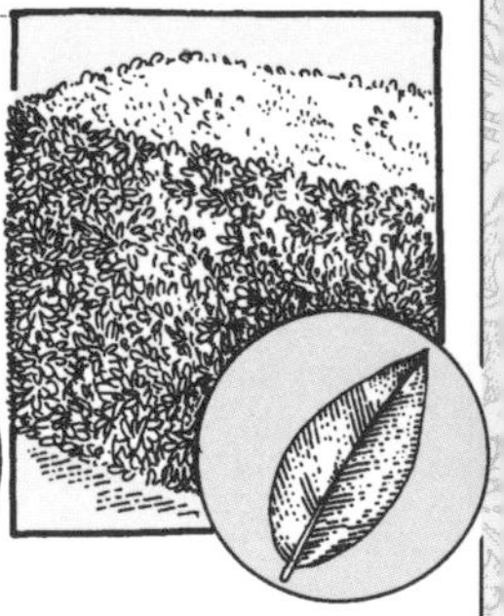

FAGUS SYLVATICA
COMMON BEECH/ EUROPEAN BEECH
Height: 3–3.6m/10–12ft
Width: 90cm–1.5m/3–5ft
Hardy deciduous tree that when planted 45–60cm/1½–2ft apart creates a formal hedge with bright green leaves, becoming dark and assuming rich yellow and russet tints in autumn. Eventually forms a tall hedge, about 5.4m/18ft.
Quick growing

LIGUSTRUM OVALIFOLIUM
CALIFORNIA PRIVET/PRIVET
Height: 1.2–1.8m/4–6ft
Width: 60–75cm/2–2½ft
*Evergreen or semi-evergreen (depending on the severity of the climate) with glossy, mid-green leaves. Set the plants 30–38cm/12–15in apart. The yellow-leaved form (*L. o. *'Aureo-marginatum') is less vigorous but more colourful.*
Widely grown

LONICERA NITIDA
CHINESE HONEYSUCKLE
Height: 90cm–1.5m/3–5ft
Width: 45–60cm/1½–2ft
Evergreen, dense hedge, ideal where little space is available. Set the plants 23–30cm/9–12in apart. Ensure the sides and top are clipped with a slight slope to encourage snow to slip off. Thick snow splays out the sides of this hedge and severely damages it.
Dense and small-leaved

THE EFFECT OF HEDGES

The wind-reducing ability of hedges – and area affected – can quite easily be calculated. For instance, on the lee side and at a distance twice the height of the hedge, the wind's speed is reduced by 75%. Reductions continue, but decrease in proportion to the distance from the hedge. Even at a distance of thirty times the hedge's height, the wind's speed is reduced.

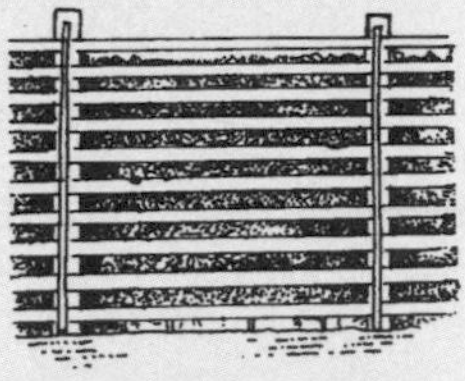

A TEMPORARY *windbreak can be effective while waiting for shelter-belt plants to become established. Form it of strips of wood nailed to posts. Double thickness wire netting also reduces the wind's speed.*

THIS *simplified (and not to scale) diagram shows how the benefit of a hedge or windbreak can be felt at a distance up to thirty times its height.*

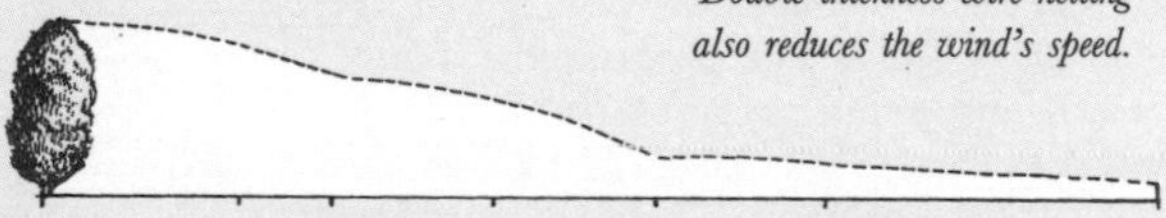

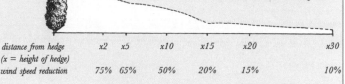

distance from hedge (x = height of hedge)	*x2*	*x5*	*x10*	*x15*	*x20*	*x30*
wind speed reduction	*75%*	*65%*	*50%*	*20%*	*15%*	*10%*

LONICERA NITIDA
'BAGGESON'S GOLD'
Height: 90cm–1.5m/3–5ft
Width: 45–60cm/1½–2ft
Evergreen, dense hedge, formed of small, yellow leaves that turn golden-green in autumn. Set the plants 23–30cm/9–12in apart. This shrub can also be grown as a specimen in a border, or against a wall where it can grow up to 1.8m/6ft tall.
Plant in full sun

PRUNUS LAUROCERASUS
CHERRY LAUREL/ COMMON LAUREL
Height: 3–4.5m/10–15ft
Width: 1.2–1.5m/4–5ft
Hardy, evergreen shrub with leathery, shiny, mid-green leaves. In spring it bears white flowers in tassels. Set the plants 45–60cm/1½–2ft apart. Some forms are smaller: 'Otto Luyken' forms a somewhat sprawling hedge.
Vigorous growth

TAXUS BACCATA
ENGLISH YEW/YEW
Height: 1.8–2.4m/6–8ft
Width: 75–90cm/2½–3ft
Dense, hardy evergreen conifer with dark green leaves. Set the plants about 45cm/1½ft apart. It is an ideal hedging shrub for forming arches – use a stiff wire frame initially to train and shape the arch. It creates a neat formal hedge, with square edges.
Slow growing

FLOWERING HEDGES

WITH FLOWERING hedges, no boundary need be bare of colour. And there are many low-growing types that can be planted as attractive internal hedges to separate one part of a garden from another.

Individual plants are planted closer together than if used as specimens in a border, so that a hedge with an even height and thick base can be created quickly. Initially, plants need to be pruned more drastically than normal to encourage bushiness from ground level. If neglected, hedges soon lose their shape and cease to be attractive garden features.

Planting hedges is detailed on pages 20 and 21.

OTHER SHRUBS

- Berberis darwinii: *evergreen; plant 30–38cm/12–15in apart; orange-yellow flowers during mid to late spring; prune after flowering.*
- Berberis x stenophylla: *evergreen; plant 45–60cm/1½–2ft apart; yellow flowers during mid to late spring; prune after flowering. Eventually it forms a wide, dense, dominant and arching hedge.*
- Escallonia: *evergreen; plant 60cm/2ft apart; range of flower colours, early to late summer; prune after flowering.*
- Rosmarinus officinalis *'Fastigiata' ('Miss Jessop's Upright'): evergreen; plant 30–38cm/12–15in apart; mauve flowers, mid-spring to late summer; trim after flowering, or prune old ones more severely in spring, when growth begins.*

ROSE HEDGES

For rose devotees hedges formed of these deciduous shrubs are an essential element of gardens. There are many to choose from – most flowering during early and mid-summer – and include:

- 'Ballerina': hybrid musk; plant 38–45cm/15–18in apart; 1.2m/4ft high; single, blossom-pink flowers.
- 'De Meaux': centifolia type; plant 38cm/15in apart; 90cm/3ft high; pure pink flowers.
- 'Little White Pet': modern shrub rose; plant 30–38cm/12–15in apart; 60cm/2ft high; small, white, pompon-like flowers.
- 'Nevada': modern shrub rose; plant 75–90cm/2½–3ft apart; 1.5–2.1m/5–7ft high; semi-double, cream-white flowers.
- 'Queen Elizabeth': floribunda; plant 60–75cm/2–2½ft apart; 1.5–1.8m/5–6ft high; clear pink, fragrant flowers.
- *Rosa rugosa* 'Frau Dagmar Hastrup': species type; plant 60–75cm/2–2½ft apart; 1.2–1.5m/4–5ft high; single, flesh-pink, delicate and very attractive.
- *Rosa rugosa* 'Roseraie de l'Hay': species type; plant 60– 75cm/2–2½ft apart; 1.5m/5ft high; rich, wine-purple, scented flowers. In autumn the round hips (sometimes called heps) become a rich orange-red.
- 'Windrush': single-flowered English rose; plant 45cm/1½ft apart; 1.2m/4ft high; lemon-yellow, fragrant flowers. Vigorous, branching growth.

FORSYTHIA x INTERMEDIA
'SPECTABILIS'
GOLDEN BELLS
Height: 1.8–2.1m/6–7ft
Width: 60–75cm/2–2½ft
Hardy, deciduous shrub with dark green leaves and masses of bright yellow flowers during spring. Set the plants 38–45cm/15–18in apart. Prune as soon as the flowers have faded.
Quick growing

FUCHSIA MAGELLANICA
'RICCARTONII'
Height: 1–1.2m/3½–4ft
Width: 60–90cm/2–3ft
Tender, deciduous shrub with red and purple flowers from mid-summer to autumn. Set the plants 30–38cm/12–15in apart. Plants are often cut down to ground level by frost. In spring, prune to soil level.
Ideal in coastal areas

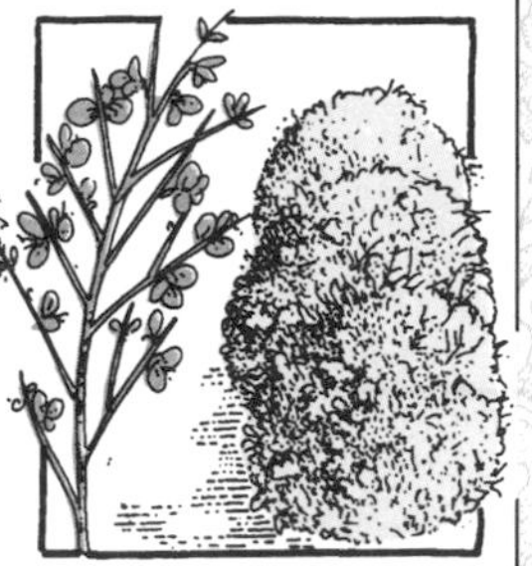

GENISTA HISPANICA
SPANISH GORSE
Height: 90cm–1m/3–3½ft
Width: 1–1.2m/3½–4ft
Deciduous, spreading shrub with golden-yellow flowers during early and mid-summer. Set plants 45cm/1½ft apart. Tends to spread: clip back after flowering. Ideal for forming a hedge at the top of a bank, when it cascades.
Slightly tender

LAVANDULA SPICA (L. ANGUSTIFOLIA/ L. OFFICINALIS)
Height: 75–90cm/2½–3ft
Width: 45–60cm/1½–2ft
Hardy, evergreen shrub with pale, grey-blue flowers from mid to late summer. Set the plants 38–45cm/15–18in apart. Clip off the dead flower heads after flowering. For a lower hedge use the well-known 'Hidcote'.
Easy to grow

POTENTILLA FRUTICOSA
SHRUBBY CINQUEFOIL
Height: 1.2–1.5m/4–5ft
Width: 60cm/2ft
Hardy, deciduous shrub with pale green leaves and buttercup-yellow flowers from late spring to late summer. Set the plants 25–30cm/10–12in apart. After flowering, clip off dead flowers.
Easy to grow

SPIRAEA x ARGUTA
BRIDAL WREATH/ FOAM OF MAY
Height: 1.5–1.8m/5–6ft
Width: 75–90cm/2½–3ft
Hardy, deciduous shrub with masses of white flowers during mid and late spring. Set the plants 38–45cm/15–18in apart. After the flowers fade, clip back the complete plant, lightly removing the flowers.
Easy to grow

SMALL CONIFERS

THESE are some of the elite of garden plants, introducing permanency to rock gardens as well as creating height contrasts in heather gardens. Many of these conifers remain miniature or dwarf throughout their lives, while others can be planted when young and moved when too dominant. Indeed, the larger ones are better in heather gardens, where they harmonize better with callunas, ericas and daboecias.

Most of these conifers are planted from containers and therefore can be set in the ground at any time when the weather and soil allow. No pruning is needed, other than cutting out vertical stems from prostrate types, or just trimming them back to prevent invasion of other plants' space.

OTHER SMALL CONIFERS

- Abies lasiocarpa *'Compacta': conical; silver-blue; height 60–90cm/2–3ft; spread 60–90cm/2–3ft.*
- Chamaecyparis lawsoniana *'Ellwood's Pillar': compact and upright; bluish-grey; height 60–75cm/2–2½ft; spread 25–38cm/10–15in.*
- Juniperus squamata *'Blue Star': compact and bushy; bright steel-blue; height 30–38cm/12–15in; spread 40–50cm/16–20in.*
- Picea pungens *'Globosa': bushy; silver-blue; height and spread 45–60cm/1½–2ft.*

ABIES BALSAMEA
'HUDSONIA'
Height: 45–60cm/1½–2ft
Spread: 50–60cm/20–24in
After about thirty years it reaches 75cm/2½ft high, often with a flattish top and formed of grey leaves that turn mid-green in midsummer. Prominent buds in winter. Other small abies include A. cephalonica *'Nana'.*
Compact and slow growing

CEDRUS DEODARA
'GOLDEN HORIZON'
Height: 60–75cm/2–2½ft
Spread: 90cm–1.2m/3–4ft
Graceful, almost semi-prostrate, dwarf conifer with a graceful habit that reveals golden branches. With age it becomes even more cascading. Cut away leading shoots that grow upwards. Position as a small focal point. With maturity, it assumes a cascade of golden shoots.
Slow growing

CHAMAECYPARIS LAWSONIANA
'MINIMA AUREA'
Height: 50–60cm/20–24in
Spread: 60–75cm/2–2½ft
Rounded, with bright yellow foliage throughout the year. Grow in full sun to retain its colour. Related small-growing conifers include 'Minima Glauca' (globular and sea-green) and 'Pygmaea Argentea' (bluish-green, tipped creamy-white).
Slow growing

CHAMAECYPARIS PISIFERA
'FILIFERA AUREA'
Height: 60–90cm/2–3ft
Spread: 60–90cm/2–3ft
Slow-growing but, eventually, grows about 3m/10ft tall. However, that need not worry most gardeners. Golden, thread-like foliage. It is ideal for planting in a rock garden, where it creates a height and colour contrast.
Eventually large

JUNIPERUS COMMUNIS
'DEPRESSA AUREA'
Height: 30–38cm/12–15in
Spread: 1.2–1.5m/4–5ft
Spreading, with bright yellow foliage in spring, bronze by autumn. Other prostrate types include 'Green Carpet' (bright green), J. virginiana *'Grey Owl' (grey-green) and* J. horizontalis *'Glauca' (steel-blue).*
Slow growing and ideal as ground cover

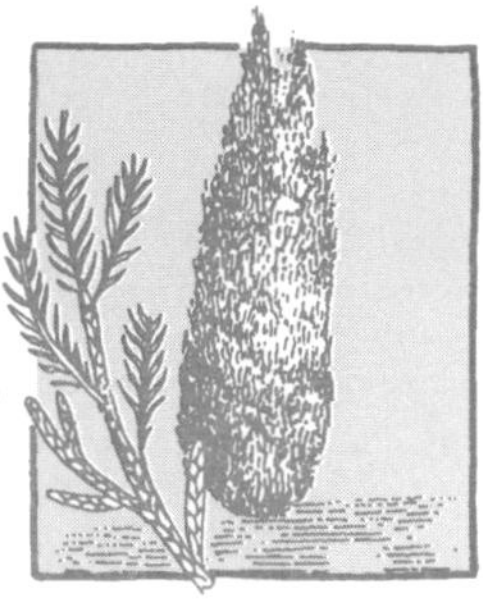

JUNIPERUS COMMUNIS
'HIBERNICA'
IRISH JUNIPER
Height: 1.8–2.1m/6–7ft
Spread: 40–50cm/16–20in
Upright and eventually forming a large shrub. Needle-like, greyish-blue foliage. Usually too large for a rock garden, but ideal in borders or heather gardens. Alternatively, try planting two either side of a path.
Slow growing

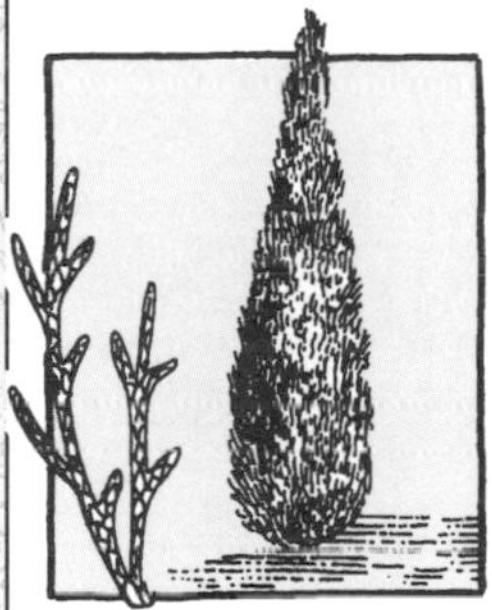

JUNIPERUS VIRGINIANA
'SKYROCKET'
Height: 1.8–2.4m/6–8ft
Spread: 23cm/9in
Narrowly upright and only 25–30cm/10–12in wide after twenty years. Scale-like, silvery-blue foliage. Ideal when planted in small groups in a heather garden. Contrasts with prostrate conifers, as well as heathers.
Columnar outline

PICEA GLAUCA
'ALBERTIANA CONICA'
DWARF ALBERTA SPRUCE
Height: 75–90cm/2½–3ft
Spread: 75–90cm/2½–3ft
Distinctive, conical outline, broadening with age and bearing dense, soft, grass-green foliage. Especially attractive in spring. It is ideal in a heather garden, or plant it in a very large rock garden.
Slow growing

THUJA ORIENTALIS
'AUREA NANA'
Height: 60–75cm/2–2½ft
Spread: 50cm/20in
Rounded, cone-shaped, with yellow-green foliage that turns gold in winter when any colour is especially welcome. It is best planted in a rock garden, although can be planted in a heather garden. Ensure it is not swamped by other plants.
Slow growing

LARGE CONIFERS

MANY conifers are so large on maturity that they cannot be considered for planting in gardens. The ones suggested here, however, are those that can be planted in gardens, either to form screens of colour or as focal points in lawns. Indeed, weeping conifers such as the Brewer's Spruce (*Picea breweriana*) need to have space around them so that the pendulous branches can be appreciated. Conversely, many forms of the Lawson Cypress (*Chamaecyparis lawsoniana*) can be planted so that eventually their foliage touches.

If you need a screen as well as a focal point at the end of your garden, plant a couple of bright yellow foliaged forms (such as 'Lanei') with the blue 'Pembury Blue' in front.

OTHER CONIFERS

- Chamaecyparis lawsoniana *'Dutch Gold': broadly conical; soft gold; height 2.1– 3m/7–10ft; spread 1.2–1.5m/ 4–5ft.*
- Chamaecyparis lawsoniana *'Pembury Blue': column-like; silvery-blue; height 1.8–3m/6–10ft; spread 1–1.2m/3½–4ft.*
- Picea engelmannii *'Glauca': pyramidal; grey-blue foliage; height 2.1–3m/7–10ft; spread 90cm–1.2m/3–4ft.*
- Pinus strobus *'Pyramidalis': narrowly pyramidal; light blue; height 2.1–3m/7–10ft; spread 1–1.2m/3½–4ft.*

CHAMAECYPARIS NOOTKATENSIS
'PENDULA'
WEEPING NOOTKA CYPRESS
Height: 6–7.5m/20–25ft
Spread: 3.6–4.5m/12–15ft
Hardy, evergreen conifer with widely-spaced branches that curve upwards at their ends. The dark green foliage has a slightly unpleasant aroma. Eventually, it grows 10m/33ft or more high.
Ideal focal point

CUNNINGHAMIA LANCEOLATA
CHINA FIR
Height: 4.5–5.4m/15–18ft
Spread: 2.4–3.6m/8–12ft
Distinctive, evergreen conifer with slightly cascading branches and glossy, dark green leaves that resemble large centipedes. It is ideal as a specimen conifer on a large lawn. Eventually, very large.
Needs a sheltered position

CUPRESSUS MACROCARPA
'GOLDCREST'
Height: 4.5–5.4m/15–18ft
Spread: 1.2–1.5m/4–5ft
Hardy evergreen conifer, with dense foliage and a narrow habit. Rich yellow, feathery, juvenile foliage. Eventually it grows 12m/40ft or more high. It is ideal for forming brightly coloured hedges in coastal areas.
Ideal in coastal areas

GINKGO BILOBA

MAIDENHAIR TREE

Height: 6–7.5m/20–25ft

Spread: 2.4–3m/8–10ft

Outstandingly attractive, deciduous conifer with leathery, fan-shaped, divided leaves, fresh green when young and darkening to green throughout summer. In autumn, they slowly become bright golden before falling.

Slow growing

PICEA BREWERIANA

BREWER'S WEEPING SPRUCE

Height: 5.4–6m/18–20ft

Spread: 3–4.5m/10–15ft

Distinctive, pendulous conifer with an attractive outline. Long curtains of shoots hang down from the branches, which characteristically turn up at their ends. The foliage is dark grey-green. Avoid cold, windy sites. A very impressive conifer.

Ideal on a lawn

PICEA PUNGENS

'THOMSEN'

Height: 2.1–3m/7–10ft

Spread: 1.2–1.8m/4–6ft

Hardy, conical, upright, evergreen conifer with branches packed with silvery-blue needles. In spring the growth is especially attractive: pale silver-blue that contrasts with the older leaves. The grey bark is also attractive.

Medium growth rate

TAXUS BACCATA

ENGLISH YEW/YEW

Height: 3.6–4.5m/12–15ft

Spread: 3.6–4.5m/12–15ft

*Beautiful hardy evergreen conifer with dark green foliage. There are several superb forms, including the Irish Yew (*T. b. *'Fastigiata') with erect growth, forming a columnar outline. In large gardens, plant in a group.*

Slow growing

GIANTS OF THE PLANT WORLD

*Few trees are as impressive as the conifers of California and Oregon. The tallest is the Californian Redwood (*Sequoia sempervirens*); one, measured in 1968, was 111m/366ft tall. Although their average age appears to be about 600, one felled in 1934 was 2,200 years old.*

*But for sheer bulk, the Mammoth Tree (*Sequoiadendron giganteum*) has no rival. It is also known as the Big Tree and Wellingtonia, having been first named* Sequoia wellingtonia, *in honour of the Duke of Wellington. Although not so tall as the Californian Redwoods, their bulk is enormous: one had a girth of 24m/79ft and a trunk volume of 1,416 cubic m/50,000 cubic ft.*

SHRUBS AND TREES FOR COASTAL AREAS

THE HAZARDS of living in coastal areas are strong winds and salt-laden sea spray, which can blow several miles inland. There are, however, many shrubs and trees that survive these conditions. Several conifers survive in front-line positions and include the Monterey Cypress (*Cupressus macrocarpa*), Corsican Pine (*Pinus maritima*) and the Austrian Pine (*Pinus nigra*). Second-line defence conifers include the fast-growing X *Cupressocyparis leylandii*, the Scot's Pine (*Pinus sylvestris*) and the Serbian Spruce (*Picca Omorika*).

Once the wind's speed has been decreased, the range of possible plants increases markedly and many of them are described and illustrated here.

OTHER SHRUBS

- Elaeagnus x ebbingei: *hardy evergreen shrub; leathery, silvery-grey leaves.*
- Euonymus japonicus: *bushy evergreen shrub; glossy, dark green leaves; many attractively variegated forms.*
- Hebe brachysiphon: *slightly tender evergreen shrub; white flowers, early to mid-summer.*
- Olearia x haastii: *hardy evergreen; white flowers during mid-summer.*
- Pittosporum tenuifolium: *slightly tender evergreen; grown for its wavy-edged leaves.*

GRISELINIA LITTORALIS
Height: 3–5.4m/10–18ft
Spread: 2.4–3.6m/8–12ft
Slightly tender evergreen shrub with leathery, thick, lustrous, apple green leaves. Ideal as a hedge or specimen shrub. There are two superb forms: 'Variegata' with leaves edged in white, while 'Dixon's Cream' has leaves splashed creamy-white. Can also be grown as a hedge.
Slow growing

HIPPOPHAE RHAMNOIDES
SALLOW THORN/ SEA BUCKTHORN
Height: 1.8–2.4m/6–8ft
Spread: 1.8–2.4m/6–8ft
Hardy, deciduous, bushy shrub – eventually 7.5m/25ft or more high – with narrow, silvery leaves. It is best known for its masses of bright-orange berries from autumn through late winter. Berries shunned by birds.
Ideal as a windbreak

OLEARIA MACRODONTA
DAISY BUSH
Height: 1.8–2.4/6–8ft
Spread: 1.8–2.1/6–7ft
Superb, evergreen shrub, with a slight musky odour. It bears holly-like, mid-green leaves and small, daisy-like flowers in tight clusters up to 15cm/6in wide during mid-summer. It survives even in extremely windy, salt-blown and exposed areas.
Slightly tender

SPARTIUM JUNCEUM

SPANISH BROOM/ WEAVERS' BROOM

Height: 1.8–2.4m/ 6–8ft
Spread: 1.8–2.4m/ 6–8ft
Hardy, deciduous shrub with rush-like green stems. The mid-green leaves soon fall off after maturing, while the pea-like, golden-yellow, fragrant flowers appear from early to mid-summer.

Quick growing

SYMPHORICARPOS ALBUS (S. RACEMOSUS)

SNOWBERRY/ WAX-BERRY

Height: 1.5–1.8m/ 5–6ft
Spread: 1.8–2.1m/ 6–7ft
Hardy, deciduous, suckering, thicket-forming shrub with mid-green leaves and small flowers during mid-summer. These are followed by white berries from early autumn to late winter. Several varieties.

Easy to grow

TAMARIX TETRANDRA

TAMARISK

Height: 2.4–3.6m/ 8–12ft
Spread: 2.4–3.6m/ 8–12ft
Hardy, deciduous shrub with pale to mid-green leaves and bright pink flowers during late spring. The whole shrub has an attractive wispy appearance. Related shrubs include T. pentandra *with rose-pink flowers.*

Survives windy areas

DYEING TROUBLE

Up to the latter part of the sixteenth century, wood was widely used to dye cloth blue. Indeed, the Saxon green, well-known during the Middle Ages, was produced by first dyeing in a weak woad solution and then with weld, a wild mignonette. And a deep purple shade could be produced if madder powder was added. Woad was therefore the universal dye of the time and woad growers had a rigid monopoly.

Indigo was used as a dye by the Egyptians and Greeks in antiquity. In the sixteenth century it was imported to Europe and Britain, deriving the name indigo as it was imported from India. This tropical shrub, Indigofera tinctoria, *proved to create a dye superior to woad. The growers of woad quite correctly envisaged the loss of their monopoly in the dyeing trade and therefore labelled Indigo 'the devil's dye'. Despite this and other edicts, especially in Saxony, it eventually became the most popular dye in Europe. During the early years of the British occupation of India, trading in indigo was very important. It was eventually replaced by a synthetic dye.*

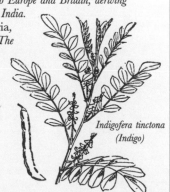

Indigofera tinctona (Indigo)

SHRUBS AND TREES FOR ACID SOILS

ACID SOILS need not be a problem for gardeners. Instead, they offer the opportunity to grow a wide range of shrubs and trees denied to gardeners living in chalky areas. And many of these acid-loving plants brighten spring with flowers in a wide range of colours. They are especially suited to shaded or woodland gardens, where dappled light filters through to them. This deciduous canopy also gives some protection from spring frosts. Additionally, these shrubs need moisture-retentive soil thoroughly enriched with peat or very well-decomposed compost.

As well as creating a glorious display of flowers, many deciduous, acid-loving shrubs have leaves that in autumn assume attractive, colourful tints.

OTHER SHRUBS AND TREES

- Camellia japonica: *late winter to mid-spring; range of colours.*
- Daboecia cantabrica: *late spring to early winter; purple-pink; also forms in white and pink.*
- Eucryphia: *mid to late summer; cream or white flowers with yellow centres.*
- Magnolia: *wide range of flowers (often fragrant), usually in spring, but* M. grandiflora *later in the year.*
- Nyssa sylvatica: *mainly grown for its richly coloured leaves in autumn.*

AZALEAS
EVERGREEN TYPES; RANGE OF VARIETIES
Height: 90cm–1m/3–3½ft
Spread: 1.2–1.5m/4–5ft
Large group of slightly tender shrubs: need shelter from cold winds and early morning sun. Funnel-shaped flowers in late spring. Some azaleas are deciduous, many having rich autumn-coloured leaves as well as flowers.
Slow growing

ENKIANTHUS CAMPANULATUS
Height: 1.8–2.4m/6–8ft
Spread: 1.2–1.5m/4–5ft
Hardy, rather upright, deciduous shrub with dull green leaves that assume rich shades in autumn. During late spring it bears creamy-white flowers with red veins in pendulous clusters. It is ideal in wild gardens, with an overhead canopy of leaves.
Slow growing

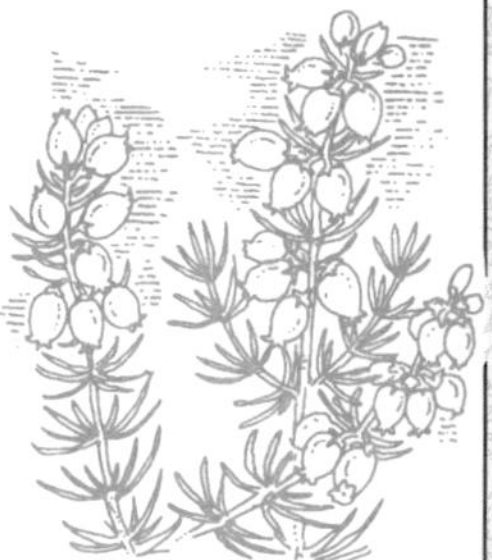

ERICA CINEREA
BELL HEATHER/ SCOTCH HEATHER/ TWISTED HEATHER
Height: 23–30cm/9–12in
Spread: 23–30cm/9–12in
Hardy, evergreen shrub with terminal flower clusters from early summer to early autumn. All ericas, callunas and daboecias grow well in acid soils, although some also tolerate lime.
Ground covering

FOTHERGILLA MONTICOLA

Height: 1.5–2.1m/ 5–7ft
Spread: 1.5–1.8m/ 5–6ft
Hardy, deciduous shrub with glossy, dark green leaves that assume rich tints in autumn. Bottlebrush shaped, sweetly scented, creamy-white flowers appear in late spring. A related species, F. major, *is not so spreading.*
Slow growing

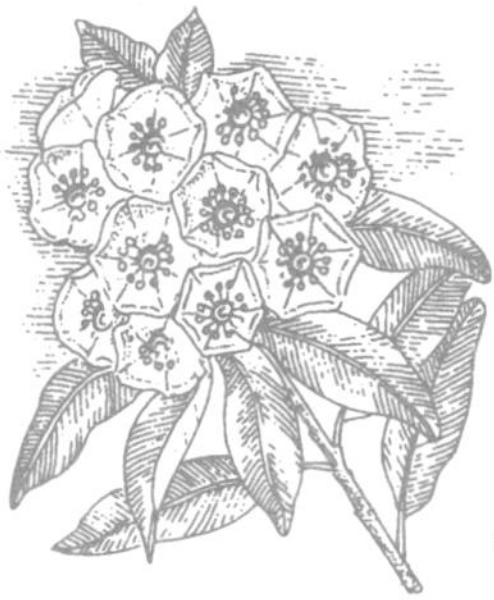

KALMIA LATIFOLIA

CALICO BUSH/ MOUNTAIN LAUREL/ SPOONWOOD
Height: 1.5–2.1m/ 5–7ft
Spread: 1.5–1.8m/ 5–6ft
Hardy, evergreen shrub with glossy, leathery, mid to dark green leaves and clusters of bright pink flowers during early summer. 'Clementine Churchill' is rich rose-red. Leaves poisonous to cattle.
Easy to grow

PIERIS *'FOREST FLAME'*

Height: 1.5–1.8m/ 5–6ft
Spread: 1.5–1.8m/ 5–6ft
Hardy, evergreen shrub, noted for its brilliant red shoots in spring that slowly turn pink, cream, then green as summer arrives. Clusters of white, pitcher-like flowers during late spring and early summer. Plant in light shade. Vulnerable to frost.
Ideal in a wild garden

RHODODENDRON

'PINK PEARL'
Height: 1.5–1.8m/ 5–6ft
Spread: 1.5–1.8m/ 5–6ft
Hardy, evergreen type with large trusses of flesh-pink flowers during spring and early summer. The wide range of other hybrids includes varieties 90cm–1.5m/ 3–5ft high. Plant in full sun or dappled sunlight, in well-drained soil.
Needs slight shade

ATTRACTING BUTTERFLIES

Scent and butterflies are a pleasing duo and several shrubs encourage their presence. These include:

- *Butterfly Bush* (Buddleia davidii): *well known for its mid to late summer flowers in several colours. Also,* Buddleia alternifolia.
- *Lavender* (Lavandula spica): *Grey-blue flowers from mid to late summer.*
- *Lilac* (Syringa): *several species, from the large-flowered types to smaller ones such as* Syringa microphylla.
- *Privet* (Ligustrum ovalifolium): *cream, heavily scented flowers in mid-summer. Mostly, the flowers on hedging plants are clipped off and therefore are only seen on free-standing shrubs.*

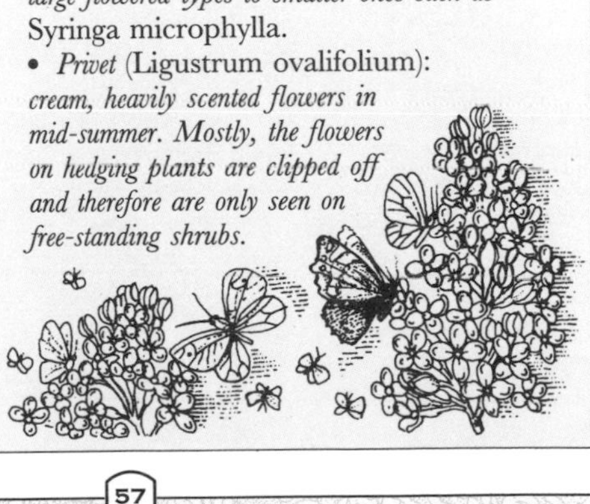

CHALKY SOILS

THERE are many shrubs, trees and conifers that thrive in alkaline soils. Although it is possible to treat localized areas within a garden with chemicals to help reduce soil alkalinity – as well as growing them in specially-prepared soil in raised beds – for long-term success it is better to choose plants that happily live in chalky soils.

When planting shrubs and trees in very chalky situations it is worth preparing the soil thoroughly. Take out a wide planting hole and dig down at least 50cm/20in to break up the subsoil. At the same time, dig in plenty of peat or well-decomposed compost. A sprinkling of bonemeal encourages rapid establishment.

OTHER SHRUBS AND TREES

- Acers: *range of species, many grown for their attractive leaves.*
- Caryopteris x cladonensis: *bright blue; mid to late summer.*
- Chimonanthus praecox: *yellow; early to mid-winter.*
- Cistus: *many species; early to mid-summer.*
- Genista: *several species, yellow and gold; late spring to mid-summer.*
- Rhus typhina: *grown for its coloured leaves in autumn.*
- Sorbus: *many species, grown for their berries.*

BUDDLEIA ALTERNIFOLIA
Height: 2.1–3.6m/7–12ft
Spread: 2.4–3.6m/8–12ft
Hardy, deciduous shrub with a cascading nature – especially when grown as a small tree – with narrow, pale-green, willow-like leaves and sweetly-scented lavender-blue flowers during early summer. 'Argentea' has hairy, silvery leaves.
Grown as a tree or shrub

CERATOSTIGMA WILLMOTTIANUM
HARDY PLUMBAGO
Height: 75–90cm/2½–3ft
Spread: 75–90cm/2½–3ft
Twiggy, low-growing shrub with small, dark green, diamond-shaped leaves that turn red in autumn. Small, rich blue flowers appear in terminal clusters during late summer. Becomes hardier with age. Can be grown in herbaceous borders.
Slightly tender

DEUTZIA x ROSEA
Height: 90cm/3ft
Spread: 90cm/3ft
Hardy, deciduous, low-growing and compact shrub with bell-shaped pink flowers on arching branches during early and mid-summer. There are several superb forms, including 'Campanulata' (white and purple) and 'Carminea' (rose-pink flowers).
Young growths in spring can be frost damaged

MOIST AND BOGGY AREAS

Some gardens have a natural high water-table, with surface soil awash in winter. Drainage is possible, but if surrounding gardens are also excessively wet there is a risk of encouraging their surplus water to pass into your garden. Do not despair as there are plants that tolerate moist and boggy soils, such as:

- *Dawn Redwood* (Metasequoia glyptostroboides): *deciduous conifer with flaking bark and mid-green leaflets that assume pink, red and brown shades before falling in autumn.*
- *Swamp Cypress* (Taxodium distichum): *also known as the Bald Cypress, this deciduous conifer has orange-brown, scaly shoots and leaves that turn russet in autumn.*
- *Willow* (Salix): *these are well known for their water-loving nature, but most are too large and invasive for small gardens. However, consider growing* Salix alba *'Chermesina' and cutting its stems back to within a few inches of the ground annually in late winter to encourage the development of brilliant orange-scarlet shoots. The shoots of 'Vitellina' are yellow.*
- *Red-barked Dogwood* (Cornus alba): *like the previous shrub, grown for its coloured stems, which are red. Other forms are 'Sibirica' with bright crimson shoots.* Cornus stolonifera *'Flaviramea' has yellow to olive-green stems.* C. s. *'Kelseyi' has purple-brown shoots.*

LABURNUM x VOSSII

GOLDEN CHAIN TREE

Height: 3–3.6m/10–12ft

Spread: 2.4–3m/8–10ft

Hardy, deciduous tree with green leaves and pendulous bunches of slightly fragrant, golden-yellow flowers in early summer. The seeds of all laburnums are poisonous, but this form does not produce seeds freely.Do not plant it near a pond.

Parts are poisonous

MALUS FLORIBUNDA

JAPANESE CRAB

Height: 3–3.6m/10–12ft

Spread: 3–3.6m/10–12ft

Hardy, deciduous tree with mid-green leaves and masses of bright carmine buds that open in late spring to reveal pale pink flowers. These are followed by yellow fruits. There are further types, with flowers and fruits in several other colours.

Forms a focal point

PAEONIA LUTEA LUDLOWII

TREE PAEONY/ TIBETAN PAEONY

Height: 1.2–1.8m/4–6ft

Spread: 1.2–1.8m/4–6ft

Shrubby, deciduous paeony with deeply segmented pale green leaves and large, golden-yellow, fragrant flowers during early summer. Slightly hardier than the normal type.

Shade from early-morning sun.

TREE AND SHRUB CALENDAR

SPRING

This has always been the season of rebirth, as well as the time for implementing plans made during winter. Shrub borders dug and prepared earlier can be planted now, using container-grown plants and balled types. It is too late for planting bare-rooted shrubs and trees as these are set in the ground during their dormant season, from late autumn to late winter when free from leaves.

The range of shrubs and trees that flower at this season is wide: specific ones are described on pages 30–31, but there are others and a few scented shrubs are featured on pages 44–45.

As well as flowers, part of the beauty of spring is the young shoots and leaves as they unfurl, although often their display lasts only for a few weeks.

- Prune all winter-flowering shrubs as soon as the last of their flowers fade (24–25).
- Prune late summer-flowering shrubs (24–25).
- Prune dogwoods (cornus) (25).
- Prune callunas and summer-flowering ericas in spring (27).
- Prune both winter and spring-flowering ericas when their flowers have faded (26–27).
- Balled plants (evergreens and small conifers) are mainly sold in spring (12–13).
- Plant balled shrubs (17).
- Container-grown plants are sold throughout the year (12–13).
- Plant container-grown shrubs when the soil allows (16–17).
- Plant balled shrubs as hedges during late spring (20–21).
- Water newly planted shrubs and trees (22).
- Transplant established evergreens in spring (22–23).

SUMMER

Summer brings warmer weather and a slight slowing in pace after nature's rush into activity in spring. But there are masses of beautiful flowering shrubs waiting to flower and many of these are described on pages 32–35. Others are better known for their coloured bark (38–39) and handsome leaves (36–37).

Hedges are important, and a range of foliage and flowering ones is suggested on pages 46–49. Conifers, both large and small, create beacons of colour throughout the year, and are described on pages 50–53.

- Dead-head large-flowered rhododendrons as soon as their flowers fade (22).
- Prune spring and early summer-flowering shrubs immediately after their flowers fade (24–25).
- Cut out water-shoots on deciduous trees as soon as they are seen (22).
- Balled plants are sold during late summer (12–13).
- Plant balled shrubs (17).
- Container-grown shrubs are sold for planting throughout the year (12–13).
- Plant container-grown shrubs, but first ensure that the soil is not dry (16–17).
- Plant balled shrubs as hedges (20–21) in late summer.
- Plant container-grown shrubs as hedges (20–21).
- Mulch all shrubs and trees, especially those newly planted, to conserve moisture in the soil and to encourage rapid establishment (22).
- Water newly planted shrubs and trees (22).
- Transplant established evergreens in late summer (22–23).

AUTUMN

This is the season of reflection, and perhaps for planning changes for the following year. It is also the time of mellow fruitfulness, with many shrubs and trees bearing colourful berries, some lasting throughout winter. A range of these plants is featured on pages 42–43, while others with richly-coloured leaves are described on pages 40–41. Some of these autumn-coloured trees and shrubs are large enough to create focal points, while others are small enough to fit into a corner.

While planning any changes, consider the soil, which may be neutral but might otherwise be acid or chalky. Check the soil with a soil-testing kit (see page 15): shrubs for acid soils are detailed on pages 56–57, while those for alkaline areas are on pages 58–59. Alternatively, use a soil pH meter: instead of having to mix soil samples with water and compare colour samples, a probe is inserted into the soil and a reading indicated on a meter. They are ideal for colour-blind people.

If the soil is moist and boggy, there are many shrubs, trees and deciduous conifers from which to choose, and some are described on page 59.

- Balled plants are sold during early autumn (12–13).
- Plant balled shrubs (17).
- Transplant established evergreens in early autumn (22–23).
- Bare-rooted plants are sold in late autumn (12–13).
- Plant bare-rooted shrubs and trees (18–19).
- Plant balled shrubs as hedges in early autumn (20–21).
- Plant bare-rooted hedges in late autumn (20–21).
- Transplant established deciduous shrubs and trees during late autumn (22–23).

WINTER

This need not be a dull season. Indeed, many shrubs flower during winter, some with scented flowers (see pages 44 and 45). Colourfully foliaged conifers, as well as those with attractive outlines, introduce further interest (pages 50–54), especially when peppered with frost or snow. Do not let snow weigh down branches on shrubs or conifers, as if it lasts for a long time they become misshapen. Use a small bamboo cane to knock off the snow gently.

The berries on some shrubs and trees last until mid or late winter, and a few of these are described on pages 42–43. For some of these shrubs to produce berries, both male and female forms are needed. For every three to five female plants, one male is needed.

Trees with colourful bark are especially welcome in winter and can be further highlighted by snow. The range of trees is wide and even includes a palm (see pages 38–39). Colourful stems are also important, as these plants are relatively small and can be fitted into most gardens (59).

- Bare-rooted plants are sold during winter (12–13).
- Plant bare-rooted shrubs and trees (18–19).
- Plant bare-rooted hedges during winter (20–21).
- Plan shrub borders in winter and thoroughly dig the soil, adding compost (14–15).
- Transplant established deciduous shrubs and trees during winter when they are dormant (22–23).
- Heel-in bare-rooted shrubs and trees in a sheltered corner if the weather is too wet or cold, or the ground frozen (19). Alternatively, put them in a frost-proof shed for a period of up to two weeks.

USEFUL SHRUB AND TREE TERMS

ACID-LOVING PLANTS: *Those that thrive in acid soils.*

AERIAL ROOTS: *Roots that grow from stems. This is a common feature with tropical trees, as well as climbers and orchids.*

ALKALINE: *Having a chalky nature and a pH reading above 7.0.*

ARBORESCENS: *Having a tree-like form.*

BALLED: *Shrubs – usually evergreens – that have been dug up and their roots wrapped in hessian prior to being sold. This method was popular before the introduction of selling plants in containers.*

BAMBOO: *A collective name for a group of plants in the grass family.*

BARE-ROOTED: *Many deciduous trees and shrubs are sold with their roots bare of soil and during their dormant season – late autumn to late winter.*

BERRY: *A fleshy, succulent fruit, such as a gooseberry.*

CALCAREUS: *Growing in chalky or limy soil.*

CALCIFUGE: *Literally lime-hating and referring to plants that cannot be grown in chalky soil.*

CALLUS: *Tissue that forms over a wound. It creates a raised surface.*

CAMBIUM: *Layer of growth and division that is just below the bark of woody stems of shrubs and trees.*

CATKIN: *A dense formation of petal-less, unisexual flowers. Some are pendent, as with hazel; others erect.*

CLONE: *A group of identical plants, all of which have been raised vegetatively from a single parent.*

COLUMNAR: *Upright and narrow. Often used to refer to some conifers.*

CONTAINER-GROWN: *Plants that are grown and offered for sale in containers.*

CULTIVAR: *A variety raised in cultivation, rather than appearing naturally without any interference from man.*

DEAD-HEADING: *The removal of faded flower heads to prevent the formation of seeds.*

DECIDUOUS: *Shrubs and trees that shed all of their leaves in autumn. A few evergreens lose some of their leaves during very severe winter weather.*

DORMANT: *A resting period, normally in autumn and winter, when a plant makes no noticeable growth.*

ENTIRE: *Complete and without indentations. A term usually used to refer to the outlines of leaves.*

ERICACEOUS: *Plants belonging to the* Ericaceae *family, including plants such as heathers, heaths and rhododendrons.*

EVERGREEN: *Plants that retain leaves throughout the year and therefore appear green the entire year. However, they regularly lose leaves, while producing further ones.*

FLOWER: *A specialized area in seed-bearing plants concerned with reproduction.*

FORM: *A loose, and rather non-botanical term used to refer to a variation within a particular species.*

FRUIT: *Botanically, a mature ovary bearing ripe seeds. Fruits can be soft and fleshy, or dry, like pods.*

GLAUCOUS: *Blue or grey-green, and usually used to describe leaves and stems.*

HEATH: *Types of* Ericaceous *plants, such as* Erica ciliaris *(Dorset Heath) and* E. tetralix *(Cross-leaved Heath).*

HARDY: *Able to survive cold, adverse weather.*

HEELING-IN: *Covering the roots of bare-rooted shrubs and trees with soil while waiting to be planted.*

H-STAKE: *A method of supporting standard trees, using two vertical stakes and one across the top, secured to the trunk.*

HYBRID: *A plant resulting from a cross between two distinct varieties, sub-species or genera. A specific hybrid is indicated by placing a cross after the first (generic) name, such as* Berberis x stenophylla.

LACINIATE: *Fringed, and usually used to describe the edges and outlines of leaves.*

LEADER: *The main stem – or several – of trees and shrubs.*

MONOTYPIC: *A genus represented by one species.*

MULCHING: *Covering the soil around trees, shrubs and other plants with well-decayed organic material such as compost.*

NEUTRAL: *Used to describe soil that is neither acid nor alkaline, with a pH of between 6.5 and 7.*

OBLIQUE STAKE: *A method of supporting the trunk of a tree. It is inserted into the ground after the tree is planted.*

PALM: *A member of the* Palmae *family and invariably native to the tropics and subtropics.*

PALMATE: *Used to describe leaves that resemble the shape of a hand.*

PETAL: *Part of a flower and, botanically, a modified leaf, usually coloured. It creates a landing place for pollinating insects as well as attracting them. When in bud, acts as a protective layer for the male and female reproductive parts.*

PH: *A measure of the acidity or alkalinity of soil, assessed on a logarithmic scale which ranges from 0 to 14, with 7 as the chemical neutral. However, most plants grow best in soil of pH 6.5.*

POLLARD: *Cutting a tree hard back to near its trunk, usually because of the lack of surrounding space.*

PRUNING: *The controlled removal of stems and shoots to encourage a plant to form a better shape and development of fruits or flowers.*

PYRAMIDAL: *Having the shape of a pyramid and often used to describe the shape of trees and conifers.*

SEMI-EVERGREEN: *A plant that may retain or lose its leaves during winter, depending on its severity.*

SHRUB: *A woody plant with several stems coming from ground level.*

SPECIMEN PLANT: *A plant that is grown on its own to create a special display or feature.*

STOOLING: *Cutting down woody stems to just above soil level to encourage the development of fresh shoots. Some shrubs and trees are regularly treated in this way, such as some willows and dogwoods.*

STANDARD: *A plant grown on a single stem, with a long, bare area between the ground and the lowest branches. Many fruit trees and roses are grown as standard trees.*

TREE: *A woody-stemmed plant with a clear stem (trunk) between the roots and lowest branches.*

TREE TIE: *A way of securing a trunk to a support. Some are plastic and proprietary, others are formed of coir.*

TRUNK: *The main stem of a tree.*

UNDERPLANTING: *Planting bulbs or small, low-growing plants under trees and shrubs to provide additional colour.*

VARIEGATED: *Mainly applied to leaves and used to describe a state of having two or more colours.*

VARIETY: *A naturally occurring variation within a plant species.*

VERTICAL STAKE: *A method of supporting a tree by inserting a strong stake vertically into the soil. It is best inserted in a hole before a tree is planted. If inserted afterwards, the roots of the tree or shrub it is supporting may be damaged.*

WEEPING: *Having a weeping appearance and used to describe the outline of a tree or conifer.*

WILD GARDEN: *An area where plants – including trees and shrubs – are grown in a controlled, semi-wild condition. Usually, there is a canopy of branches overhead to create shade and protect plants from frosts, especially in spring.*

INDEX

Abies balsamea 50
Acacia 37
Acer 11, 36, 38, 40
Acid soil 15, 56–7
Amelanchier 30
Arbutus 26, 38, 42
Artocarpus communis 6
Aucuba 26, 42
Autumn, leaf colours 11, 40–1
Azaleas 56

Balled plants 12, 17, 20, 62
Bamboo 35
Banks, Sir Joseph 6
Bare-rooted plants 12, 18–19, 20, 62
Bark 11, 38–9
Beech 46
Berberis 26, 30, 48
Berries 11, 42–3, 62
Betula 38
Borders 14–15, 32
Box 26, 46
Breadfruit 6
Broussonetia 9
Buddleia 10, 11, 24, 44, 57, 58
Butterflies 57
Butterfly bush 10, 24, 25, 44
Buying shrubs 12–13

Calendar 60–1
Calico Bush 26
Callicarpa 42
Calluna 27, 36, 52
Camellia 30, 56
Caryopteris 34, 58
Catalpa 36
Cedrus deodara 50
Ceratostigma 59
Chaenomeles 31
Chalky soils 15, 58–9
Chamaecyparis 50–2
Chimonanthus praecox 24, 28, 44, 58
Chlorosis 15
Choisya 26, 44
Cinchona calisaya 8–9
Cistus 10, 32, 58
Clark, W. 6–7, 29
Clematis 7
Climate 10–11, 54
Coastal areas 54–5
Coca 8
Cocoa 9, 43
Coconut palm 9
Coffee 8, 9, 41
Coloured,
bark 11, 38–9
leaves 11, 36–7
shoots 25, 38–9
stems 25
Commercial uses 8–9
Conifers 16, 50–3
Containerized plants 12, 16–17, 20, 62
Cork Oak 9
Cornelian Cherry 28
Cornus 24, 28, 38
Corylus maxima 37
Cotinus 36–7
Cotoneaster 11, 42
Cotton 45
Cunninghamia 52
Cupressocyparis 54
Cupressus 52
Cypress 52, 54, 59
Cytisus 31

Daphne 28, 42, 44
Dead-heading 22, 62
Deciduous type 11, 16, 18–20, 24–5, 62
Deutzia 32, 58
Dichopsis guttata 8
Drugs 8, 9

Elaeagnus 7, 11, 54
Elaeis guineensis 9
Enkianthus 7, 56
Erica 27, 28–9, 56
Escallonia 34, 48
Eucalyptus 39
Eucryphia 34, 56
Euonymus 37, 54
Evergreen type 11, 16, 20, 26–7, 62

Fagus sylvatica 46
Fever Bark Tree 8, 9
Fibres 9, 45
Ficus elastica 8
Flowers 25, 39, 62
hedges 20, 48–9
Forsythia 24–5, 49
Fothergilla 44, 57
Fruits 31, 42–3, 62
Fuchsia 34, 49

Garden centres 12–13
Garden shops 13
Garrya elliptica 10
Genista 49, 58
Ginkgo biloba 53
Glossary 62–3
Golden Bells 24–5, 30, 49
Gorse 30, 31, 45, 49
Gossypium 45
Griselinia 36, 54
Gum trees 39, 40–1
Gutta-percha 8

Hamamelis 24, 29, 44
Heather 27, 28–9, 56
Hebe 32, 54
Hedges 20–1, 46–9
Hevea brasiliensis 8
Hibiscus 7, 35
Hippophae 42, 54
Honeysuckle 46–7
Hydrangea 7, 10, 35
Hypericum 35

Indigo 55

Joshua Tree 27
Juniperus 50–1

Kalmia 26, 57
Kerria japonica 31
Koelreuteria 40
Kolkwitzia 33

Laburnum 44, 59
Laurel 26, 47, 57
Lavender 27, 49, 57
Leaves, coloured 11, 25, 36–7, 40–1
Lewis, M. 6–7, 29
Ligustrum 46, 57
Lilac 7, 45, 57
Liquidambar 40, 41
Lone-bushes 33
Lonicera 28, 46–7

Magnolia 7, 23, 31
Mahonia 6, 28–9, 42
Maidenhair tree 53
Mail order 12, 13
Malus 42, 59
Maple 11, 36, 38, 40
Metasequoia 59
Mexican Orange Blossom 26, 44
Mock Orange 25, 32, 37, 44
Mulberry 9
Mulching 22, 63
Musa paradisica 9

Nurseries 12, 13

Olearia 26, 54

Paeonia 33, 58
Palaquium gutta 8
Palm trees 9, 38, 63
Paper 9, 27
Parrotia persica 40
Pernettya 43
Philadelphus 25, 32, 37, 44
Picea 50–1, 52–3, 54
Pieris 30, 57
Pinus 54
Planning 14–15, 60–1
Plantain 9
Planting,
balled plants 17, 20
bare-rooted plants 18–19, 20
containerized plants 16–17, 20
hedges 20–1
Potentilla 32, 49
Preparation 14–15, 18, 20, 21
Privet 46, 57
Pruning 24–7, 63
Prunus 26, 30, 39, 47
Pyracantha 43

Quercus suber 9
Quince 31

Range available 10–11
Redwood trees 53, 59
Rhododendron 26, 57
Rhus typhina 40–1, 58
Ribes 25
Robinia 36–7
Rosemary 45, 48
Roses, as hedges 48
Rubber tree 8

Salix 59
Sambucus racemosa 37
Scented varieties 11, 15, 28, 44–5
Senecio 33
Sequoia 53
Shoots 25, 38–9
Shrubs 11, 63
origins 6–7
Skimmia japonica 43
Snowberry 6, 55
Soils,
acid 15, 56–7
chalk 58–9
testing 15
wet 59
Sorbus 43, 58
Spartium junceum 55
Spiraea 49
Spring-flowering shrubs 25, 30–1
Staking 17, 18–19
Stems 25, 59
Sumach 40–1, 58
Summer-flowering shrubs 25, 32–5
Symphoricarpos 6, 55
Syringa vulgaris 45

Tamarisk 25, 55
Taxodium 40, 59
Taxus baccata 47, 53
Theobrama cacao 43
Thuja orientalis 51
Trachycarpus 38–9
Transplanting 22–3, 27
Trees 11, 38–9, 63
origins 6–7

Ulex 30, 45

Variegated plants 11, 20, 63
Viburnum 7, 29, 42

Wardian cases 7
Water-shoots 22
Watering 17, 21, 22
Weigela 25, 33
Willow 59
Wind protection 17, 21, 47
Winter Sweet 24, 28, 44, 58
Winter-flowering shrubs 24, 28–9
Witch Hazel 24, 28–9
Woad 55

Yew 23, 47, 53
Yucca 9, 27, 34